C000180190

GRAN TURISMO

Huw Evans

MOTORBOOKS
INTERNATIONAL

DEDICATION

As my first work, I would like to dedicate this book to all my friends and family and to every true automotive enthusiast and avid driving game fanatic on the planet.

ACKNOWLEDGMENTS

It wouldn't have been possible to produce *The Cars of Gran Turismo* without the help of the following: Jerry Heasley, John Russell, and Ken Nord for their outstanding photography; Jon Day at the National Motor Museum (U.K.) Picture Library and Tim Wright at LAT/Autosport for supplying some very hard-to-find automotive and motorsport pictures; and Kathy Farrell of *Auto Express/Evo* magazine, for providing me with such an abundance of quality and dramatic photography, and whose contribution really helped take this work to another level. I would also like to thank Lee Klancher and Peter Bodensteiner at MBI for listening to my rantings and deciding to publish one of my ideas, to Glenn Barie of Granturismobynumbers.com for his help with the gamer contributions, and finally to Mark Hughes at Haynes Publishing, who introduced me to the world of special interest publishing, for which I am forever grateful.

This edition first published in 2003 by Motorbooks International, an imprint of MBI Publishing Company, Galtier Plaza, Suite 200, 380 Jackson Street, St. Paul, MN 55101-3885 USA

© Huw Evans, 2003

All rights reserved. With the exception of quoting brief passages for the purposes of review, no part of this publication may be reproduced without prior written permission from the Publisher.

The information in this book is true and complete to the best of our knowledge. All recommendations are made without any guarantee on the part of the author or Publisher, who also disclaim any liability incurred in connection with the use of this data or specific details.

We recognize that some words, model names and designations, for example, mentioned herein are the property of the trademark holder. We use them for identification purposes only. This is not an official publication.

Motorbooks International titles are also available at discounts in bulk quantity for industrial or sales-promotional use. For details write to Special Sales Manager at Motorbooks International Wholesalers & Distributors, Galtier Plaza, Suite 200, 380 Jackson Street, St. Paul, MN 55101-3885 USA

Library of Congress Cataloging-in-Publication Data

Evan, Huw, 1975-
  The Cars of Gran Turismo / by Huw Evans.
    p. cm.
  Includes index.
  ISBN 0-7603-1495-0 (pbk. : alk paper)
  1. Gran Turismo (Game) I. Title.

GV1469.35.G73E83 2003
794.8--dc21

On the front cover: Pagani's Zonda is perhaps the ultimate in millennium supercars with its gorgeous space-age styling and unbelievable performance. *AutoExpress/Evo*

On the frontispiece: Nissan's Skyline, unavailable in the United States and scarce everywhere but Japan, is one of the most popular cars in Gran Turismo. *John Russell*

On the title page: Japanese Grand Touring Car racing provided the inspiration for Gran Turismo. Here, a Mugen Honda NSX leads the Toyota Autobacs MR-S at the Mount Fuji circuit. *Ken Nord*

On the back cover: Part of Gran Turismo's appeal lies in the extraordinary variety of vehicles that players can drive. Pictured (from top to bottom) are Mitsubishi's amazing Lancer Evo VII in one of its natural habitats. *John Russell*; Nissan's awe-inspiring and ultra-quick Skyline GT-R V-spec. *AutoExpress/Evo*; Aston Martin's wonderful Vantage supercar. *AutoExpress/Evo*; and one of the highly successful Spoon Sports-prepped S2000s that compete in Japan's Super Taikyu Endurance series. *John Russell*

About the author: Huw Evans was born in Wales and now lives near Toronto, Canada. He edited the comprehensive reference work *Hot Cars*, served a stint at *Essential Superbike* as technical editor, and currently freelances for *High Performance Pontiac*, *Muscle Mustangs and Fast Fords*, and *Classic American*. He bought his first Playstation in 1998 and a copy of Gran Turismo soon followed.

Edited by Peter Bodensteiner
Designed by LeAnn Kuhlmann

Printed in Hong Kong

CONTENTS

INTRODUCTION

Since Gran Turismo appeared in late 1997 for the original Sony PlayStation, Polyphony Digital's driving simulator masterpiece has become a household name. While many driving simulators came before Gran Turismo, most of them were either very broad or narrow in focus, often with marginal results. None gave gamers the right balance of vehicles, tuning options, circuits, racing scenarios, and playability. Many suffered from poor graphics and were too complex.

When Gran Turismo arrived on the scene, it blew every other driving game into the weeds. It distinguished itself with some of the best graphics ever seen. It provided accurate renderings of real production cars that most people could relate to or at least aspire to drive some day. To some, Gran Turismo's most outstanding aspect was its excellent replay feature, which was so good it was like watching a race on TV.

What made the game more than just another light and sound show, however, was its in-depth simulation. The cars in the game sounded and even drove like the real-life cars. Gamers were required to earn a series of licenses in order to drive more powerful cars, adding to the game's challenge. In Arcade mode, a truly entertaining multiplayer feature allowed friends to race each other.

Gran Turismo was a hit from day one. The predictable flood of imitators followed, but few came close to matching the original. Gran Turismo was also significant as the first driving game auto enthusiasts embraced on a huge scale, thanks in part to the technical attention to detail by the game's authors. Shortly after Gran Turismo's arrival on the market, many car shows and racing

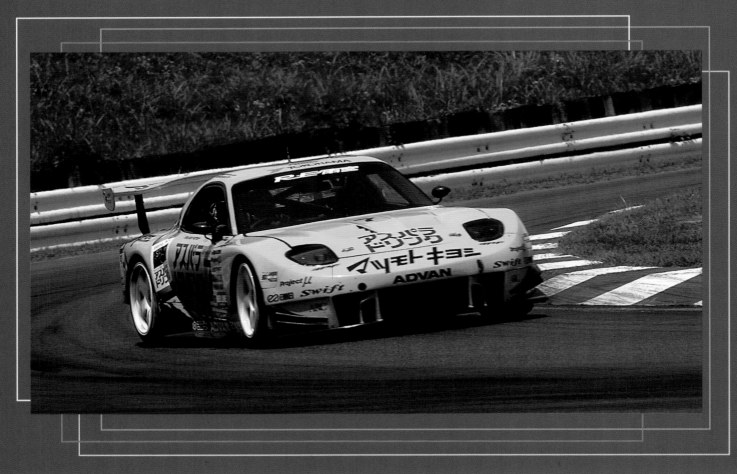

events were populated by full-size vehicles clearly tuned and styled after their virtual counterparts. Some of these events even had "new wave" bench-racing wars, with enthusiasts linking up their car-mounted PlayStations for duels on the Deep Forest or High Speed Ring Raceways. Gamers would use their virtual tuning garages to tweak their game rides for maximum performance and, ultimately, virtual victory.

As Gran Turismo fever swept across the globe, fans clamored for an updated version. When GT2 appeared in 1998, many breathed a sigh of relief that it hadn't strayed too far from the original's successful formula. It did, however, add more cars (over 500), more tracks, and a rallying element—which only served to broaden the game's appeal.

When Sony introduced a second-generation console— PlayStation 2—Gran Turismo loyalists wondered whether GT creator Kazunori Yamauchi and his team at Polyphony Digital would release another version of a now definitive driving simulator. The initial plan was to release GT3 (to be called Gran Turismo 2000) in Japan in late 1999, timed with the Japanese launch of PS2. The new version, however, was delayed by nearly two years.

When GT3 A-spec (a term synonymous with highly tuned cars in Japan) was introduced, it was clear that the extra time bubbling in the pot ultimately resulted in an even better product. GT3 showcased fewer cars than

GT2 (still more than 150 different vehicles from around the world), but it took the game to a whole new level in terms of graphics, content, and playability. It even offered an iLink feature, enabling players to hook up six different PS2 consoles and televisions for seriously competitive racing.

As I pen these words, there hasn't been much word on a successor to GT3, though a couple of spin-off (and very clever) GT Concept games have been released. These enable players to race one-off exotic and concept cars that most of us will never see in the flesh.

Speaking of virtual cars, the Gran Turismo series also gave many gamers and enthusiasts some insight into truly world-class performance vehicles, like the Nissan Skyline GT-R, Mistubishi Lancer Evolution, and Subaru Impreza WRX, which previously had been little-known outside Japan. One can argue that Gran Turismo is largely responsible for the current surge in global popularity of these vehicles. Manufacturers have introduced versions of these cars for official sale in Europe and North America, where once they were reserved exclusively for Far Eastern customers.

Gran Turismo has introduced many Western enthusiasts (and the public) to the world of Japanese high-performance automobiles and tuning. It has also provided a window into the world of modern European and Far Eastern sports/touring car

racing and rallying, as well as exposure to a few lesser-known (and independent) automotive marques that regularly field vehicles in these events with considerable success.

The objective of *The Cars of Gran Turismo* is not only to give both gamers and enthusiasts an insight into this popular and colorful game and the culture surrounding it, but it is also to provide an analysis of some of the awesome machines that inspired Gran Turismo, many of which have never been seen before in this format. To that end, this book is dedicated to every Gran Turismo player and auto enthusiast on the planet, and I hope you enjoy reading it as much as steering a virtual Nismo 400-R Skyline or Lancer Evo VII around Mid-Field Raceway or Special Stage Route 11.

—Huw Evans
Barrie, Ontario
Canada

Gran Turismo has forever changed the way many people look at driving simulators and the world of performance cars. Currently in its third mainstream incarnation, Gran Turismo has spawned an entire subculture that is alive and well from Milan to Tokyo. Even today, despite the introduction of newer games, it remains the benchmark by which all other driving sims are judged.

A NEW BREED OF DRIVING SIMULATOR

Gran Turismo started off as the idea of a man who loved cars, racing, and video games. Kazunori Yamauchi wanted to create the ultimate driving simulator, with realistic driving conditions and cars that would appeal to gamers and auto enthusiasts of all ages. This

new simulator would be the best of its kind.

As a producer for software company Polyphony Digital, Yamauchi and his team went to work, approaching Polyphony's parent company, Sony, about the idea for the new game. Sony's top brass agreed, thinking that the game would be a good companion to their new generation game console, PlayStation.

In late 1997, when PlayStation went on sale in Japan, one of the key games available for it was Gran Turismo. Upon inserting this unassuming-looking driving game into their freshly purchased consoles, gamers were simply blown away. The combination of graphics, attention to detail, cars, circuits, and playability were utterly amazing. The fantastic replay

In-car entertainment reached new levels in the 1990s when people installed not only killer stereo systems, but also LCD displays with DVD players and game consoles like in this 2001 Mustang Cobra convertible. Many second-generation gaming devices like PS2 play movies as well as video games.

feature took the concept of virtual-reality automobile racing to a new level. Squint your eyes and you could almost be watching a real motorsports event on the tube.

PlayStation hit North America, Europe, and other markets soon afterward. The combination of PlayStation and Gran Turismo had the same mesmerizing effect. Gran Turismo appealed not only to avid gamers but also to car enthusiasts. Many gearheads had never really played a driving simulator before, but they got hooked on Gran Turismo simply because it was so utterly detailed and realistic.

From there, Gran Turismo fever spiraled to new heights. Players put together game forums on the Web, creating

In GT3 particularly, the number of racing machines is quite staggering. Some are derived from Le Mans racers while others are based on machines that compete in the Japan Grand Touring Car Championship (JGTC). These Honda NSXs are seen at the Mount Fuji circuit in 2002. *Ken Nord*

HOW I GOT HOOKED ON GRAN TURISMO
"I saw the original at a friend's house in July 1998 and knew I just had to have it. The graphics and detail of the cars were nothing like I'd ever seen before. The way the cars handled was like no other game simulation. And watching those instant replays was like watching TV—I have a strong interest in sports car racing and this aspect blew me away."
*GB24hours, U.S.A.
Owner, GranTurismo by Numbers*

Most of the major factories in Japan have their own competition departments or affiliates. MazdaSpeed, Mugen (Honda), Nismo (Nissan Motorsports), and Toms (Toyota Motorsports) build, service, and race high-horsepower versions of their top-line street cars. *Ken Nord*

HOW I GOT HOOKED ON GRAN TURISMO
"It was word of mouth—people were talking about the finest racing game ever. I tried it; it was the start of a very beautiful love affair."
Skiddo, U.K.

virtual racing championships and posting their game results on competitive league tables after each session. Recognizing that many people were now buying PlayStations simply to get their hands on Gran Turismo, Sony offered special packages, including memory cards, additional controls, and a range of games as standard along with the console. In Japan, Polyphony Digital entered the world of real auto racing, sponsoring several teams in Japanese road racing events.

In the automotive aftermarket, PlayStation installations in cars and SUVs became the next big thing in in-car entertainment. At many custom car shows, races, and events, people of all ages and backgrounds raced against each other in their cars without even starting the engine.

On top of the already-growing sport compact boom,

tuning Japanese-style became the next big thing, particularly in the United States and Canada. Aftermarket parts suppliers began to peddle Japanese-style lowering kits, ground effects, monster tires, exhaust systems, turbocharger kits, and various Japanese Domestic Market (JDM) components to an increasingly hungry audience. Magazines like *Super Street* amplified the trend, covering Japanese road racing and the country's tuning scene as a way of conveying the future of automotive tuning to their readers.

Probably not in their wildest dreams did Polyphony Digital or Sony realize just how much of an impact Gran Turismo

HOW I GOT HOOKED ON GRAN TURISMO
"Initially, it was the sheer number of cars featured in GT2 and the ability to change the performance of each one by upgrading and replacing various components."
Andy, U.K.
www.racing-line.org

would have on popular culture around the world. Best of all, the game accomplished this largely on its own merits, not via media and advertising hype. Just as TV shows and movies had influenced popular culture over the years, it was now time for video games to take over—and Gran Turismo was leading the charge.

THE ORIGINAL: GRAN TURISMO

Gran Turismo managed to achieve such universal appeal by accomplishing things that no other racing or driving simulator had before.

The best part of the game is the driving dynamics of the cars. Each car is based on a full-on production machine, accelerating, handling, and braking in a manner reminiscent of the real thing. With a number of different circuits to race on—from high-speed ovals to tight street courses—some vehicles are better suited than others. A player must utilize each car's particular strengths in order to post the quickest lap times and win the race—just as in real motor racing events. Engine sound effects closely mimic each car, as each vehicle's sounds were developed from actual recordings.

The stunning "camera angles" and detailed animation also make Gran Turismo so captivating. Each car is instantly recognizable as a real-life machine, right down to the lights, windshield wipers, and correct-pattern wheels. The animation is incredibly fluid. The cars squat under acceleration, dive under braking, and lean through the corners, just like their real-world counterparts. The tracks are incredibly detailed, and so is the scenery, right down to flashing cameras in the grandstands and prominently placed sponsor logos of actual companies throughout each course.

The sounds just add to the fun. You can hear your tires squeal and the crowd's roar as you drive by the virtual spectators. Each race is also accompanied by a killer music score from real-life recording artists—not just creations of the software company, like many other games.

After each race, a replay feature lets you watch your progress. Not only is it amazing to view, but it enables players to learn from their mistakes and assess their strengths and weaknesses in certain cars and through particular sections of each course.

The white, red, and green Castrol Tom's race-prepped Supra competes in the JGTC. Toms is one of Japan's veteran tuning facilities and has worked its magic on countless Toyota street cars over the years—everything from Celicas to Chaser and Mk II sedans. *Ken Nord*

The game gives you a choice of either Arcade or Simulation mode, each appealing to different kinds of gamers. In Arcade mode, you can race against five AI (artificial intelligence) drivers on your own, by yourself against the clock, or against a colleague in two-player mode. The Arcade races last a few laps, and you can choose from a variety of different cars and different levels of difficulty.

As much fun as the Arcade mode is, it is in the Simulation mode where the real genius in Gran Turismo can be found. In Simulation mode, each player starts out with a small amount of money (displayed in credits), which gives you a selection of

Among the most-dominant vehicles in JGTC are the Nismo-prepped Skyline GT-Rs. *Ken Nord*

MAD ABOUT CARS

"I've been an automobile fan my whole life but never did much more than local drag racing. I've had nearly 40 cars so far, and I've always driven them pretty hard. There are certainly a lot of similarities in how the cars in the game react compared to real life, which is part of its fascination. That reminds me, I must head out to the local autocross."

Basement Paul, U.S.A.

This Calsonic-sponsored Skyline is the real-life counterpart to one of the cars featured prominently in Gran Turismo 3. *Ken Nord*

entry-level cars from which to choose. Once you have your car, you take the licensing test. Each license you earn enables you to enter a certain category of racing. Winning a race gives you more credits, which you can use to buy a better car or tune your existing one.

The tuning option lets you upgrade every aspect of the car, from wheels and tires to engine,

RELEVANCE TO THE REAL WORLD
"I have a strong interest in racing and performance driving. The game won't teach you how to drive a real car, necessarily, but the techniques you learn about analyzing the track, your performance, and that of the car will be applicable to any kind of racing."
Random, U.S.A.

exhaust, brakes, driveline, and suspension. Tuning alters the driving characteristics of each car, so Gran Turismo lets you test your latest setup via a "machine test" or on the track

prior to taking the next license or trophy race. This allows you to make adjustments to best suit the track and driving conditions—just as real racers do. No other racing game on the planet offers that same kind of detail in its tuning options.

The more licenses you earn and the more cup races you win, the more credits you obtain. This enables you to purchase better and faster cars (there are four different parts of town where you can shop for a new ride), and tune them to an insanely high level to simply clobber the competition. Upon completion of a certain level, players can unlock a new prize car free of charge, which they can add to their Home Garage on the menu screen. The more levels a player completes, the more interesting the prize cars—and the more difficult the tournaments. Whether progressing through Simulation mode or playing the quick races in Arcade mode, Gran Turismo provides hours of virtual racing fun!

In Japanese Touring Car racing, regulations stipulate that the cars must be loosely production-based, thus you will find many recognizable shapes from Far Eastern streets, like this Silvia, dicing it out on the track. *Ken Nord*

(VIRTUAL) REALITY EXPERIENCE
"I started playing GT1 at university. I used to crash at a friend's place after a night out, and the following morning turned into several hours of playing GT1 or GT2 on his brother's PlayStation. I got hooked. Later, I got the GT3 Racing Pack as a gift and played it a lot.

"I found www.granturismobynumbers.com in mid-2002 through my activities moderating on automotive Web forums. As a result of meeting the numbers, I now meet with a group that plays locally in Auckland on a weekly basis for iLink racing. We even did a demonstration at the opening of a local speed shop.

"I've been lucky in that I've driven a lot of the cars featured in GT in real life and have a good working knowledge of them. Therefore, I can see the game as a very well thought-out and fantastically done simulator. Some cars behave better and are more accurately depicted than others, but overall, GT is amazing. However, like most things, it shouldn't be taken too seriously—fun is the name of the game."
Moppie, New Zealand

Regulations in the JGTC also require that the teams base their power plants on essentially stock engines. Most of these motors crank out around 500-plus horsepower in racing tune. *Ken Nord*

GRAN TURISMO 2

With the success of the initial Gran Turismo, work soon began on a successor. Gran Turismo 2 emerged in late 1999 and appeared at first glance to be essentially a rerun of its trailblazing predecessor. It added a significant number of improvements, however. The game's imagery was smoother, with more depth to the cars and scenery. GT2 came as a two-disc set, and the list of cars was drastically increased. Players could now choose from well over 500 different makes and models. Whereas the first game had a heavy bias toward Japanese machinery, GT2 offered a huge variety of cars of all ages from around the globe—everything from a tiny Daihatsu Cuore TR XX up to a thundering 1969 Chevy Camaro Z28. The variety of circuits was

also increased to a total of 27 different tracks, up from nine on the original release.

A big plus was the addition of a rally section. For racing on the rally circuit, you could either use some of the specific rally cars offered or choose to build your own car. You could race against the clock, like in real World Championship Rallying, or play against a friend in Arcade mode.

Simulation mode featured simplified menu choices and a very clever feature that enabled you to convert your license passes from GT1 to GT2 via data transfer and a PlayStation memory card. Unlike GT1, many of the racing series in Simulation mode had strict entry requirements, including restrictions on engine power, for more evenly matched racing and greater realism. GT2

possessed an amazing soundtrack with a greater number of songs, many by contemporary artists. As in GT1, the songs were perfectly tuned to the fast-paced world of motor racing, whether actual or virtual.

GRAN TURISMO 3 A-SPEC

Originally conceived merely as an enhancement of the first two games, the third edition of Gran Turismo became a great deal more than that. Initially titled Gran Turismo 2000, the name was later changed to Gran Turismo 3 A-spec.

When Sony began developing an improved PlayStation 2, it was only natural that one of the games designed for it would be a version of the now legendary

ONLINE ADVENTURES

"Before I got into Gran Turismo, I was an avid gamer. Racing games were always at the top of my list, though I thought many of them didn't live up to their potential. After getting my hands on Gran Turismo, with all of its cars from the real world, I knew it was created for people like myself. My favorite aspect was the ability to drive what you wanted, from hatchbacks to F1 cars—that is something special, and it contributes to GT's enduring popularity.

"I had always entertained the idea of creating a website, but my only problem was the lack of a suitable topic or subject. Then I got GT2. On a whim, I decided to start a community of my own to see what I could do. Naturally, I thought GT2 would make an excellent topic that I would enjoy working with. After a year of server limitations, I wanted to do more with my website and the online community that revolved around it. I registered my own domain name, found some real hosting, and launched GTPlanet.net.

"Supported by enthusiastic members from the old site, www.GTPlanet.net hit the ground running and we haven't looked back. As the launch of GT3 A-spec drew near, our website was receiving literally thousands of hits. After upgrading the website's server to accommodate all the newcomers, the online GT community was free to expand to its fullest potential without any sluggish pages or technical limitations. Since then, GTPlanet.net has become home to exclusive content and multimedia—it was even featured in the May 2002 issue of *Sport Compact Car* magazine. The future is only looking better for Gran Turismo enthusiasts, with the release of GT Concept and (hopefully soon) GT4. I'm glad that GTPlanet.net is there to be a part of all this excitement."

Jordan, U.S.A.
Owner, GTPlanet.net

Gran Turismo series. Polyphony Digital Executive Producer Yamauchi and his team had planned to release this new version in time for the original PS2 launch, but the added complexity of the PS2 brought with it new challenges, which took a while to overcome.

When GT 3 A-spec finally arrived on the shelves in spring 2001, many aficionados were disappointed at first. After all, it only had 150-plus cars. But once people started playing the new game, they realized that this was far more than a rehashed version of GT2. GT3 retained all the goodies that made its predecessors so popular, but it leveraged the infinitely more powerful PS2 console to deliver far greater graphic definition, detail, and smoothness. The cars and circuits looked more lifelike than ever.

Although the choice of vehicles was drastically reduced (due to the added time it took to reproduce each of them on PS2 software), there was a greater number of actual racing machines, including Le Mans cars. Additional circuits included the Complex String test course and the magnificent Cote d'Azur (the classic Monaco Grand Prix circuit in all its glory). The five AI racers in single-player Arcade or cup races now reacted more like actual humans, making silly mistakes under pressure and driving aggressively for a more realistic simulation.

GT3 also featured 10 endurance races and a huge number of championship events—some of which took as long to complete as real Grands Prix! An iLink mode enabled gamers to hook up six individual consoles and televisions to play a full-fledged competition of their own. Sadly, an actual online gaming option wasn't available, though Yamauchi, and his team at Polyphony hinted that this might arrive for the next major incarnation of Gran Turismo.

Of all the improvements in GT3 A-spec, perhaps the biggest jewel in the crown was the existence of six ultra-secret, full-fledged Formula 1 prize cars, which players could unlock upon completion of certain levels. Like the rest of the cars in the game, these were based on actual F1 machines that ran from the mid-1980s through the mid-1990s. There was even a specific F1 Grand Prix championship. In order to race in it, players had to complete all 40 beginner and amateur cup races.

GT3 was, in every sense of the word, a proper sequel and a huge improvement over the previous two versions. A tremendous amount of credit must be given to Kazunori Yamauchi and his team for not resting on their laurels. They created an even better driving simulator and took the video game masterpiece that is Gran Turismo to the next level.

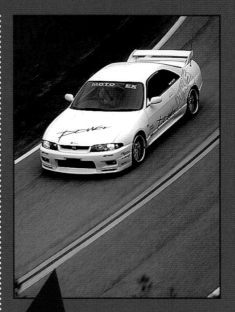

Gran Turismo gave many of us a new spin on the world of tuning and modifying cars—Japanese style. One of the most favorite platforms with which to build street machines is Nissan's R33 incarnation of the Skyline. Bigger and heavier than its R32 predecessor, the extra girth didn't mean it was slower. The rear- and all-wheel drive coupe versions became just as popular with tuners as their predecessors. *John Russell*

The RB26DETT engine found in the more sporting Skylines could be tuned to deliver ludicrous power levels—900 bhp wasn't an impossibility. Just getting all those horses effectively to the tarmac was the hard part. *John Russell*

13

TUNING

One of the most interesting and clever aspects of Gran Turismo is the ability to tune and modify each and every car at your disposal. This fact alone makes it unique among racing simulators on the market. It also illustrates a keen sense of awareness and enthusiasm among the game's production team for real-world tuning companies.

The idea of making cars go faster, handle and look better has been around forever. But as a result of Gran Turismo, many companies (particularly those in the Far East) have been brought to the attention of auto enthusiasts around the globe. In Japan, companies such as Bozz, C-West, HKS, MazdaSpeed, Mugen, Nismo, Spoon, and Toms have built some amazing machinery over the years—everything from dedicated Time Attack and Drift specials to high-performance daily drivers. The kits and tuning options offered by these companies directly inspired the smorgasbord of tuning parts in Gran Turismo. In turn, Gran Turismo helped transform vehicles tuned in this traditional Japanese style into global superstars—many of these hot rods have since been emulated on the street and immortalized in magazines, TV, and film.

Subaru offers a full range of STi-based models in Japan, including the Legacy and Impreza (shown). Although the latter was primarily conceived for conquering dirt and loose gravel, it can be built into a tremendously entertaining street/track machine. This one, tuned by Bozz Speed, is based on the lightweight RA rally conversion car and will literally scare the daylights out of all but the most hardened drivers. *John Russell*

Factory Subaru Impreza WRX STi engines are rated at 276 bhp in this (EJ20) form. That hasn't stopped tuners like Bozz from coaxing considerably more power from them and—with a little ingenuity and patience—400-plus reliable horsepower is quite possible for a street-driven Impreza. This particular engine features an STi spec C turbocharger, special Bozz exhaust, bigger intake, and front-mounted oil cooler, among other things. *John Russell*

LOOKING TO THE FUTURE
"We have a feeling that although no one from Polyphony Digital has yet contacted us directly, they know about the online community and get a feel about what goes on and what people are looking for. Hopefully, future versions will incorporate real-time online play with your own customized cars."
GB24hours, U.S.A.
Owner, Gran Turismo by Numbers

SECTION 2: THE CARS

In Gran Turismo, perhaps like any TV series or motion picture relating to automobiles, the cars are the real stars. What makes the game so amazing is the level of detail that went into each individual model. The contours, stance, and dynamics of each vehicle are spot-on in almost every instance. What is also impressive is the sheer variety of vehicles. From little superminis, such as the Toyota Vitz/Yaris, to the fire-breathing, V-12–engined Lister Storm, each has its place and its fans. This is not only true in the virtual automotive universe, but in the real one too. One essential ingredient unites these cars—every one is truly exhilarating to drive.

CLASS C

The entry-level category in the game, known as Class C, basically contains vehicles most of us can relate to every day. It's a good place to start both in Arcade and Simulation mode, as these vehicles are good platforms to gain track experience. As in the game, each is supremely tweakable, and, depending on the amount of time and money invested, you can create something rather quick and unusual.

CLASS B

After you have a few laps under your belt and have obtained your first competition license and earned a few credits, it's time to step up a notch. Class B vehicles get a bit more expensive and sporty. These vehicles are still worthy of being daily drivers, but they place greater emphasis on sporty styling and road manners than the vehicles featured in Class C.

CLASS A

Some seriously fast machinery appears in Class A. These cars are equally at home blasting along the expressway or a winding, two-lane country road as they are ripping it up on the drag strip or road course. Most of these vehicles cost considerably more than those featured in Class B, both in Gran Turismo credits and in real-world dollars, euros, or yen.

CLASS S

It's time to enter the big leagues. To drive these cars in GT3 A-spec, you'll need to get your Super License and earn a serious amount of credits. In the real world, things aren't much different: You'll need either a considerable amount of influence or a fairly extensive background in professional-level motorsport.

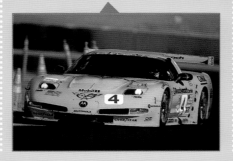

RALLY CARS

Gran Turismo added this new category of racing with the release of GT2, and it returned, better than ever, for GT3 A-spec. In place of smooth road courses, we found ourselves piloting AWD monsters through the dust and mud of the Smokey Mountains, the Swiss Alps, and the rudimentary Tahiti Circuit. In fact, two of the greatest stars of all three Gran Turismo games owe their origins to the real-life rally circuit—the Mitsubishi Lancer Evolution and Subaru Impreza WRX STi. Rallying has been popular in many parts of the world for decades, and, thanks in part to Gran Turismo, the sport is finally making serious inroads in North America too.

PRIZE CARS

Some of the most exciting cars of Gran Turismo are the ones you can win after completing the required races in Simulation mode. As you progress through the game, the tournaments and cup races become more difficult. As a result, the vehicles you can earn become ever more exciting.

TOYOTA VITZ 1.5

Built on a single basic platform, yet sold in different guises around the world—Vitz (Japan), Yaris (Europe), and with a trunk as the Echo (U.S.)—this attractive little car was conceived as a replacement for the Starlet and Tercel and arrived on the scene late in 1998.

Offered in two- and four-door versions, it features extensive use of lightweight materials, which gives it an excellent power-to-weight ratio and good fuel economy. Offered with 1.2- and 1.5-liter, four-cylinder engines packed with up-to-the-minute technology and an unusual dash with central mounted speedometer and gauges, it's a fun, entry-level car in standard trim, but nothing too (dare we say it) exciting.

However, there have always been a sizeable number of individuals who want a vehicle just a little bit more sporting than your average run-of-the-mill family car. In this case, Toyota built a pumped-up version of the pint-sized people mover, which it labeled the Vitz 1.5 RS/Yaris T-Sport. It features the same basic architecture and powertrains as the other models, but received a hotter 107 bhp version of the twin-cam 1.5-liter, all-alloy four-cylinder, along with stiffened suspension, quicker steering, and a more precise gearbox. Weighing in at just 960 kg, this little rocket will rush from 0–60 in a fairly respectable 9.4

When Toyota unveiled its latest pint size "world" car, it was only natural that a more sporting version would arrive on the scene. The resulting Vitz 1.5RS/Yaris T-Sport was based on the three-door hatchback and gave entry level buyers a dose of driving excitement for an attractive price. *AutoExpress/Evo*

Key to the Vitz/Yaris' spritely performance is the 1.5-liter four cylinder, which features dual overhead camshafts and Toyota's VVT-i (variable valve timing and electronic fuel injection). *AutoExpress/Evo*

TOYOTA VITZ 1.5 RS/YARIS T-SPORT
SPECIFICATIONS *

Weight	2,116 lbs/960 kg	0–60 mph	9.4 sec
Layout	FE I-4 NA FWD	0–100 mph	32.8 sec
Displacement	1.5 liters	Top speed	115 mph
Max power	107 bhp @ 6000 rpm	Years in production	2000–
Max torque	107 lb/ft @ 4200 rpm	Cost in Gran Turismo credits	14,530
Transmission	5-speed manual		

*refers to T-Sport

"FUN LITTLE CAR. WOULD BE NICE IF THEY SOLD IT HERE IN THE U.S."
RANDOM, U.S.A.

The unusual dash features a central-mounted gauge cluster. The 1.5 RS and T-Sport versions feature a touring style three-spoke wheel and the addition of a tachometer in the instrument pod. A five-speed manual gearbox was standard. *AutoExpress/Evo*

Outwardly the RS/T-Sport is distinguished from other Vitz/Yaris models by standard alloy rims, lower profile tires, fog lights, rocker extensions, and front and rear spoilers. *AutoExpress/Evo*

seconds and reach the magic 100 mph mark in just 32.8, yet still returns 40.9 mpg on the highway. If that isn't enough (especially if you live in Japan), you can always take your Toyota to your local Toms (Toyota Motor Sports) mechanic—the real-world equivalent of the Gran Turismo tuning garage!

MINI COOPER

Although now replaced by its much-hyped successor, it would be unwise to dismiss the original Mini as a has-been. After all, if it hadn't been for the tremendous success and universal appeal of this little car, it is extremely doubtful its bigger replacement would be sold adjacent to BMW franchises today.

Conceived by the late Sir Alec Issigonis, this revolutionary little car burst upon the scene in 1959 and was initially available in two versions: badged as an Austin or Morris. Although excellent in its own right, it took the involvement of racing supremo John Cooper to really turn this car into a legend. Cooper took the basic Mini, dropped in a bigger 1,275-cc version of its four-cylinder A-series engine, bolted on a low-restriction exhaust, tweaked the hydroelastic suspension, and added fatter wheels and tires on 10-inch wheels. Presto! The original sport compact was born.

Weighing in at 730 kg with an excellent power-to-weight ratio, low center of gravity, and fantastic handling, the Mini 1.3 Cooper S would give fits to drivers of bigger, more powerful machinery. The car's exceptional performance and agility not only made it a legend on the street but on the racetrack too. Minis took part in several road racing series and even rallying with great success—Paddy Hopkirk, Roger Clark, and others drove

An all-time classic, the original Mini is one of the most recognized automotive symbols around the world. After an absence of two decades, a sporty Cooper version returned to the line in 1990. *AutoExpress/Evo*

With an available Union Jack roof decal and driving lights, the reborn Mini Cooper was Charlie Croker and *The Italian Job* all over again. *AutoExpress/Evo*

the little cars to numerous victories in events like the Monte Carlo and Swiss Alpine rallies during the 1960s.

With the renewed interest in everything sixties by 1990, which included a rebirth in

British performance, the Rover Group (which at this time was building Minis) reintroduced the Mini Cooper. Like the sixties original, this re-born version was available in traditional colors such as British Racing

1.3 S

MINI COOPER 1.3 S
SPECIFICATIONS

Weight	1,609 lbs/730 kg	0–60 mph	12.2 sec
Layout	FE I-4 NA FWD	0–100 mph	n/a
Displacement	1.3 liters	Top speed	90 mph
Max power	63 bhp @ 5500 rpm	Years in production	1990–2000
Max torque	70 lb/ft @ 3000 rpm	Cost in Gran Turismo	
Transmission	5-speed manual	credits	16,900

"PUT SIX PEOPLE IN THESE AND HEAD OUT TO AN ILINK RACE, HEEHEE. AWESOME HANDLING."
RANDOM, U.S.A.

A major result of progress was a more inviting cabin with gauges mounted directly ahead of the driver. The classic Mini driving position with bus-angle steering wheel remained, however, as did the characteristic long shifter. *AutoExpress/Evo*

strong. On the open road, this latest version was every bit as entertaining to drive as its illustrious predecessor and still retained the essential character that defined the Mini from day one. The reborn Cooper lasted right up until the end of original Mini production

in 2000. The final versions offered grille-mounted driving lights along with fender flares and beefier wheels and tires, adding a mean, hunkered-down rally look and even better handling.

green, with optional Union Jack roof decal and sixties-style "Minilite" alloy wheels. It also featured a 1,275 engine (now fuel injected), upgraded exhaust, and tighter suspension, but it boasted comfort and convenience features that could only have been dreamed of 30 years before. Demand for the new Cooper version proved very

The "new" Cooper 1.3i S was built in both left- and right-hand drive versions, but the vast majority were sold in the United Kingdom and Japan from 1990–2000. *AutoExpress/Evo*

ALFA ROMEO

When Alfa Romeo launched its replacement for the boxy 155 in 1997, its new front-drive mid-sized 156 was worthy of the title of world's most beautiful sedan. Styled by an in-house team headed by Walter Da Silva, the new 156 boasted very elegant, fluid lines. Cleverly hidden rear door handles, which gave it the side profile of a two-door coupe, were an interesting touch. Other trademark styling cues included a traditional Alfa Romeo grille (the boldest one seen in years and signifying the Milan company's return to greatness) along with attractively curved bumpers and an offset front license plate.

Inside, the 156 was just as attractive, with a distinctive twin-pod dash and sporty three-spoke steering wheel. In longstanding Alfa tradition, the 156 boasted all-independent suspension, vented four-wheel disc brakes with ABS, and a choice of fuel injected 1.6-, 1.8-, and 2.0-liter four-cylinder engines. The latter engine incorporated Alfa's patented Twin Spark Technology.

With all these ingredients, the car proved an instant hit and deservedly garnered the prestigious European Car of the Year award for 1998. Since then, Alfa has introduced a 2.0-liter Selespeed model (with steering wheel-mounted F1-style paddle shift controls), a

When the Alfa 156 burst upon the scene in 1997, there was nothing like it. So taken were the Europeans by this new sedan that they bestowed the prestigious car of the year award upon it. *AutoExpress/Evo*

sport wagon, and V-6 version. The V-6 is a new 2.5-liter, DOHC (dual overhead cam), all-aluminum engine that cranks out 190 bhp and is teamed with a six-speed manual gearbox.

Save for standard front driving lights and differently patterned wheels, very little distinguished the V-6 version from its lesser stablemates, though many buyers ordered the optional "Sport Pack," which added perimeter body extensions and a massive decklid wing for a more sporting appearance. Fast, refined, and beautiful handling, the V-6 was finally eclipsed in 2002 with the launch of a new flagship for the 156 range: a homologation special called GTA (after some of the company's great racing/sports/touring cars).

Silky-smooth 2.4 valve -V6 engine and quick-shifting six-speed transmission make the Alfa Romeo 156 2.5 a true delight. *AutoExpress/Evo*

The GTA, built as a counterpart to the 156s, raced in European touring car events, is powered by a bigger 3.2-liter V-6, and

156 2.5 V6

ALFA ROMEO 156 2.5 V6
SPECIFICATIONS

Weight	2,970 lbs/1,347 kg	0–60 mph	7.3 sec
Layout	FE V-6 NA FWD	0–100 mph	n/a
Displacement	2.5 liters	Top speed	142 mph
Max power	190 bhp @ 6300 rpm	Years in production	1998–
Max torque	164 lb/ft @ 5000 rpm	Cost in Gran Turismo	
Transmission	6-speed manual	credits	38,910

"GREAT LITTLE CAR; A LITTLE UNDERPOWERED BUT LOTS OF POTENTIAL."
MOPPIE, NEW ZEALAND

Inside, the 156 combines both classic and modern style with distinctly Italian flair and good ergonomics. Deeply recessed gauges are a throwback to the great Alfas of the 1960s and 1970s. *AutoExpress/Evo*

The Sport Pack, seen on this car, adds aero extensions and a decklid spoiler. Many V6 models are fitted with it, but the pack is available for the entire 156 sedan range. *Auto Express/Evo*

features a beefed-up suspension and transmission, quicker steering, and some unique exterior and interior trim pieces. With 0 to 60 times of around six seconds flat, it is also the quickest 156 yet, and it will no doubt enhance the already successful 156 lineup.

MAZDA MX-5

In the late 1980s, traditional-style sports cars seemed a bit passé. Many buyers who bought open-top roadsters a decade or two before were now happier motoring around in plush, closed-roof GTs, with leather seats, air conditioning, and cruise control.

Then in 1989 Mazda launched a slinky sports car in Japan called the Eunos Roadster. An export version called the MX-5 Miata soon followed and created a huge splash, particularly in the United States and Europe. Like the original European machinery (notably the best-selling MGB), the MX-5 had all the right ingredients. It was sexy and stylish, a manageable size (something that mattered in many parts of the world), and handled great. Best of all, it was affordable.

Furthermore, unlike many classic sports cars of yesteryear, the MX-5 was reliable and had a good-fitting convertible top and a heater that actually worked. It proved a sellout success, causing other manufacturers to follow

Prior to the launch of this car, there was little choice when it came to affordable and true sporting open motoring. Five years after the debut of Mazda's Miata, there was an abundance of baby sports cars to choose from. *AutoExpress/Evo*

suit with their own variations of the "new wave" sports car. It was cool to be topless once again.

Mazda did it by applying the back-to-basics principle. The engineers in Hiroshima took a close look at the elements that made the MGB and others so popular: a lightweight and well-balanced chassis, compact dimensions, and rear-wheel drive. The engineers also eliminated anything that would add weight, complexity, and cost.

What emerged was a small and light convertible (it weighed only 950 kg) with gorgeous, up-to-the minute styling. Underneath, the new car had a very stiff unibody (for the time) and true sports car-style suspension, with double wishbones at all four corners. The only engine offered was a 1.6-liter, dual overhead cam four cylinder, which cranked out 116 bhp and transmitted power to the 14-inch rear wheels via a five-speed manual gearbox.

Although power output was modest, even by late 1980s' standards, the MX-5 was simply a revelation on the open road. No, it wasn't particularly fast (0–60 mph took 9.4 seconds), but superbly accurate steering and fantastic poise made the little sports car a delight to pilot through corners.

Originally available in only red, blue, and white, and with

In the United States and Canada, the MX-5 was dubbed "Miata," which means "prize." In Europe it was simply called MX-5 and in Japan the car was sold under the Eunos brand as the Roadster. *AutoExpress/Evo*

MIATA (EUNOS ROADSTER)

MAZDA MX-5 MIATA (EUNOS ROADSTER)
SPECIFICATIONS

Weight	2,094 lbs/950 kg	0–60 mph	9.4 sec
Layout	FE I-4 NA RWD	0–100 mph	n/a
Displacement	1.6 liters	Top speed	118 mph
Max power	116 bhp @ 6500 rpm	Years in production	1989–1993
Max torque	114 lb/ft @ 5000 rpm	Cost in Gran Turismo	
Transmission	5-speed manual	credits	17,000

> "GREAT LITTLE CAR. GOOD PLATFORM WITH WHICH TO LEARN AND HONE YOUR SKILLS. ONE OF MY FAVORITES FOR LAGUNA SECA."
> IY, CANADA

Packing just 116 bhp, the 1.6-liter engine was peppy if not exactly powerful, but combined with quick steering and light weight, it made for one entertaining drive and a great foundation for novice drivers who wished to master the art of oversteer. *AutoExpress/Evo*

Pop-up headlights were standard on all first-generation MX-5s and gave the car a distinctive face when in use. Even today, the lines of this little machine still look attractive. *AutoExpress/Evo*

few optional extras, it wasn't long before Mazda tinkered with the basic formula. A limited edition, complete with British Racing Green paint and a tan interior, went on sale for 1991 as a homage to U.K. sports cars of old. In 1994 Mazda installed a bigger 1.8-liter engine with 130 bhp and revised the suspension. Purists said this changed the MX-5's character, and, despite being quicker, the later versions just didn't have the same delicate poise and balance that made the 1989–93 models so captivating.

AUDI TT

Spun off the incredibly versatile Audi A3/MK IV Golf Platform, the TT is named after the great pre-war Tourist Trophy races of the 1920s and 1930s in which the great silver Auto Unions (Audi's predecessors) competed. First shown as a motor show concept in the early 1990s, the slinky little 2 + 2 coupe proved an instant hit with the public, which led Audi to develop a full-scale production version.

Initially available with a 180 bhp 1.8-liter turbocharged four-cylinder engine, standard five-speed manual gearbox, and a choice of front or all-wheel drive (Audi's patented Quattro system), the coupe was a success from the start, though problems soon surfaced. Responding to criticism from the automotive press that the car was underpowered and didn't handle as well as it

Although the original 180 bhp five-speed TT was an excellent automobile (particularly in post-1999 form), its more powerful 225-horse stablemate transformed the little car into a serious performer. *Jerry Heasley*

should, Audi revised the TT in 1999. They altered the suspension and added a small rear spoiler to provide greater downforce. This spoiler spoiled an otherwise pure design, but

without it, the car's clamshell shape had a tendency to produce lift and upset the car's handling.

The folks at Ingolstadt also added a more powerful 225 bhp version, which offered a six-speed gearbox (later offered on the 180hp car) and bigger 17-inch wheels and tires. It was this version that really put the TT on the map as a world-class sports machine—now it had some serious power to back up the excellent chassis and stunning looks.

Speaking of looks, the coupe was joined by a gorgeous two-seat roadster in mid-2000. Audi was fairly quick to enter the TT in competition—notably in the prestigious DTM (German Touring Car) series. Both its prowess on the racetrack and

With 0–60 mph times quicker by almost a second, plus even better handling and outstanding grip in Quattro form, the more powerful motor turned Audi's image builder into essentially a baby Porsche Carrera 4, and the public loved it. *Jerry Heasley*

AUDI TT
SPECIFICATIONS

Weight	3,075 lbs/1,395 kg	0–60 mph	6.1 sec
Layout	FE I-4T AWD	0–100 mph	16.7 sec
Displacement	1.8 liters	Top speed	150 mph
Max power	225 bhp @ 5900 rpm	Years in production	1999–
Max torque	206 lb/ft @ 2200 rpm	Cost in Gran Turismo credits	46,580
Transmission	6-speed manual		

> "STUNNING MACHINE AND NOT AT ALL BAD FOR A CLASS B MACHINE. DOESN'T HANDLE AS WELL AS IT SHOULD, THOUGH."
> — UNKNOWN

All TTs have a well-thought-out interior with controls logically placed. Chrome embellishments such as the dash vents, gauge trim, shifter boot housing, and steering wheel add a touch of teutonic class. *Jerry Heasley*

on-road performance and style ensured that it remained a consistent favorite with the motoring press and public. The TT also did an excellent job boosting showroom traffic as well as reviving Audi's once flagging image around the globe.

Built at a dedicated assembly plant in Hungary, the TT is arguably one of the finest expressions of automotive design to emerge during the late 1990s, and will no doubt become a future classic. *Jerry Heasley*

If there is one automobile that personifies the entry-level Gran Turismo-style street/track racer, it is the 1997–01 Integra Type-R.

On the outside, save for Type-R badging and a more prominent rear spoiler, there is little to indicate this three-door hatchback isn't your everyday grocery getter. Once you get behind the wheel, however, your perception instantly changes.

This little screamer employs a 1.8-liter DOHC four-cylinder with Honda's legendary VTEC variable valve timing. It makes its maximum 195 horsepower at a peaky 8,000 rpm and emits a very raspy exhaust note. This is combined with ultra-crisp steering, a quick-shifting gearbox, big brakes, and stiffened suspension (which helps give it virtually uncompromised handling). The Type-R makes

At the time of its introduction, the Type-R's 1.8-liter DOHC engine was just about the most powerful normally aspirated production four cylinder in the world. *John Russell*

every trip to the store seem like a Touring Car race. In fact, the Type-R proved a very successful racer at the grassroots level in America, backing up its race-inspired engineering with on-track results.

If you wanted an affordable track-style thrill ride during the late 1990s, this was where the buck stopped. Further accentuating the Type-R's racer-style character is the fact that early versions came in any color you wanted, so long as it was white (Japan's national racing color) with contrasting red interior. Due largely to the popularity of this little rocket, The Type-R badge rose from obscurity to become one of the most coveted emblems in the automotive performance market—a tradition that continues to this day.

Key ingredients to the Type-R's incredible handling and track prowess were all-around double wishbone suspension, ultra-stiff unibody, and a pair of massive 11.1–inch diameter front brakes taken directly from the NSX supercar. *John Russell*

ACURA/HONDA INTEGRA TYPE-R
SPECIFICATIONS

Weight	2,427 lbs/1,101 kg	0–60 mph	6.2 sec
Layout	FE I-4 NA FWD	0–100 mph	17.9 sec
Displacement	1.8 liters	Top speed	145 mph
Max power	195 bhp @ 8000 rpm	Years in production	1997–2001
Max torque	130 lb/ft @ 7300 rpm	Cost in Gran Turismo	
Transmission	5-speed manual	credits	25,160

> "GREAT REPLICATION OF THE REAL CAR, BUT SUFFERS FROM THE UNDERSTEER BUG INHERENT IN ALL GT3 FWD CARS. KEEP IT LIGHT AND LEAN TO GO AROUND DEEP FOREST II."
> MOPPIE, NEW ZEALAND

Noisy, thrashy, and hard riding, the Type-R wasn't among the most civilized of its genre around town, but give it a twisty two-lane open road and all was forgiven. *AutoExpress/Evo*

As initially launched, the Type-R was a dedicated street/track racer, with minimal interior sound deadening and no air or radio. Early cars came only in white, but colors were later expanded for broader market appeal. *John Russell*

One of the most underrated cars of its genre (and era), the Fiat Coupe was an excellent car and a brave stab by Italy's largest automaker at the GT market, something the Turin-based company hadn't tried for years.

Launched in 1993, the Coupe was built on the same platform as the boxy Tipo front-drive hatchback, but its dramatic styling looked like nothing else. Actually designed in-house by Fiat, the cars were assembled by Pininfarina. In fact, the famed Italian coachbuilder's name appeared on the rocker panels behind the doors and on the dash.

Beneath the dramatic coachwork, engine choices were a 2.0-liter, dual overhead cam, 16-valve four cylinder with 142 bhp, plus another 2.0-liter four—a 196 bhp turbocharged version (borrowed from the

Few contemporary cars on sale in Europe were as striking as the 1993–2000 Fiat Coupe. And few offered the same fun-to-drive qualities at a similar price. *AutoExpress/Evo*

Lancia Delta Integrale). Teamed with a standard five-speed gearbox, the Fiat Coupe Turbo was a spritely performer, but the best was yet to come.

In 1997, the Turin company introduced a new line of five-cylinder 20, valve engines, which naturally found their way under the Coupe's hood as a substitute for the previous four bangers. Despite being the same overall displacement (2.0 liters), the additional cylinder and four valves made a world of difference in the performance stakes. The five-cylinder Coupes were much more torquey than their predecessors and incredibly fun.

Normally aspirated Fiat Coupes could hit 60 mph in 8.3 seconds, but the 220-horse turbo model proved the hot ticket and was largely responsible for bringing ear-to-ear grins to anyone who got behind the wheel. This version could reach the magic 60 mph mark in 6.4 seconds and go on to a top speed of 155 mph. Despite having so much power transmitted to the front

Inside, the Coupe was remarkably spacious for its size, especially up front. Five speeds were standard at first, though six forward gears arrived in 1998. *AutoExpress/Evo*

20V TURBO

FIAT COUPE 20V TURBO
SPECIFICATIONS

Weight	2,881 lbs/1,307 kg	0-60 mph	6.4 sec
Layout	FE I-5T FWD	0-100 mph	n/a
Displacement	2.0 liters	Top speed	155 mph
Max power	220 bhp @ 5750 rpm	Years in production	1997-2000
Max torque	228 lb/ft @ 2500 rpm	Cost in Gran Turismo	
Transmission	5-speed manual	credits	21,030

> "VERY FAST FOR A FRONT DRIVER, EVEN BEFORE A STAGE 1 TUNING. CAN BE TRICKY IN THE CORNERS THOUGH."
> UNKNOWN

Pininfarina emblems were carried on the rocker panels, but the unique design was actually done by Fiat in house. Pininfarina was tasked with production of the Coupe unibodies.
AutoExpress/Evo

Bolting on a turbocharger to the Fiat Coupe's 20-valve five-cylinder engine resulted in a very respectable 220 bhp and dragster-like acceleration.
AutoExpress/Evo

wheels, the turbocharged Coupe was a decent handler. It was wise to exercise caution through fast corners, however, as torque steer made the car a bit tricky at the limit. But who could really complain about torque steer when you had gorgeous styling and near-supercar acceleration for the same price as a boring family sedan! The only real downside to the Fiat Coupe Turbo was that production ceased in 2000, and not nearly enough of them were built.

HONDA CIVIC

First seen in 1973, the Civic has matured to become one of the world's most popular and best-loved economy cars. Prior to the 1990s, though, the Civic rarely found itself in the same sentence with the word "exciting."

However, after several successful Grand Prix endeavors and the introduction of the NSX supercar, Honda began applying some of its "race inspired" technology to the entire lineup, which at the time was decidedly less than sporting. At the entry-level end of things, what better place to start than with the Civic?

By fitting a tuned 1.6-liter four-cylinder engine and

A best-selling economy car around the world, the Civic benefited greatly from Honda's racing exploits. The 2002 incarnation of the Type-R packed a powerful 197 bhp 2.0-liter four with the latest I-VTEC variable valve timing. *AutoExpress/Evo*

Like its Integra predecessor, the Civic Type-R's motor didn't come into its own until it hit 6,000 rpm on the tach. Its peaky power characteristics and ultra-stiff unibody made it a great weekend club racer. *AutoExpress/Evo*

uprating the suspension and brakes, Honda created the first truly sporty factory Civic—the Si-R. By 1997, the Si-R had become the Civic Type-R and, like its Integra stablemate, was available only in white.

Fast forward to 2001. With Type-R mania in full swing across the globe, Honda launched its latest Civic Type-R. Using the stiff three-door British-built hatchback, Honda's engineers installed a high-revving, 197 bhp 2.0-liter DOHC 16-valve iVTEC four cylinder. Mated to it is a six-speed manual gearbox with very short throws. Other differences from the standard Civic Si hatch include an uprated suspension with stiffer

TYPE-R

HONDA CIVIC TYPE-R
SPECIFICATIONS

Weight	2,654 lbs/1,204 kg	0–60 mph	6.8 sec
Layout	FE I-4 NA FWD	0–100 mph	16.9 sec
Displacement	2.0 liters	Top speed	146 mph
Max power	197 bhp @ 7400 rpm	Years in production	2001–
Max torque	145 lb/ft @ 5900 rpm	Cost in Gran Turismo	
Transmission	6-speed manual	credits	19,980

"IN SOME RESPECTS, IT'S BETTER THAN THE INTEGRA, BUT NEEDS A STAGE ONE EXHAUST BEFORE IT CAN ACTUALLY PULL AS WELL AS THE REAL CAR."
MOPPIE, NEW ZEALAND

springs and firmer shocks, plus bigger front disc brakes and stronger front and rear anti-roll bars. Outwardly, the 2002 Civic Type-R sports a mesh grille with a unique front air dam and rear hatch spoiler, along with discreet Type-R emblems.

Honda's engineers spent a considerable amount of time thrashing development Type-Rs around Germany's famous Nürburgring circuit, and the result is a great-handling little car that is exceedingly entertaining to drive. The little

Civic Type-R is capable of accelerating from 0 to 60 mph in less than 7 seconds and covering the quarter in around 15.4 at 88 mph.

Inside, the Civic Type-R boasted white-faced instrumentation and six-speed gearbox with the shifter mounted high up on the console. *AutoExpress/Evo*

All 2002 Civic Type-Rs were three-door hatchbacks built exclusively at Honda's plant in Swindon, Wiltshire, England—even those destined for sale in Japan! *AutoExpress/Evo*

MITSUBISHI FTO

In perhaps typical Japanese-to-English lexicon, the initials FTO stand for Fresh Touring Origination. While its name may be a bit awkward, this pretty and rare coupe remains one of the world's great surprises.

When it burst upon the scene in October 1994, the FTO's distinctive styling was received well enough to earn it the Japanese car of the year title. Spun off the same platform as the evergreen Lancer/Mirage, the Japanese Domestic Market (JDM)-only FTO came in three distinct guises with a choice of power plants. The entry level GS was powered by Mitsubishi's 1.8-liter four cylinder, with the step-up GR featuring a 2.0-liter V-6.

It was the GPX version that got the most interest, however. This model featured the 2.0-liter V-6, but with MIVEC (Mitsubishi Innovative Valve Timing and Electronic Control) and 197 bhp. Teamed with either a five-speed manual (rare) or clever INVECS II five-speed tiptronic-style gearbox (which features a manual "sport" mode and will learn a particular driver's shifting preferences), the GPX is a quick little pill. Sixty arrives in 6.7 seconds and top speed is around 140 mph.

As good as it is in a straight line, it is corner carving that makes the FTO such a great machine. Although it boasts rather pedestrian struts and trailing arms, the chassis and

Prior to the original release of Gran Turismo, few people outside of Japan had any idea what the FTO was. Since then, interest in the little front-drive coupe has been gaining around the world. *AutoExpress/Evo*

suspension are dialed in to perfection. Despite being front-wheel drive (Gran Turismo offers a four-wheel drive FTO, but in reality it was never built for production), the car is so balanced and well-behaved through the turns that you tend to forget which set of tires the power comes from on all but the most slippery of roads.

In 1997, the FTO received a handsome facelift and a longer list of standard comfort and convenience options, including ABS brakes, twin airbags, and traction control in an effort to broaden its appeal. However, production sadly ceased in 2000, with the ultimate version being the now highly

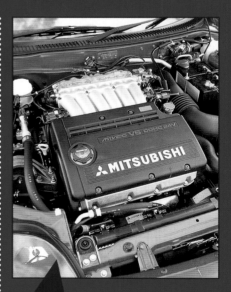

The most exciting variant was the GPX/GP-R version, with its intriguing 2.0-liter MIVEC V-6. This featured four valves per cylinder and variable valve timing. Above 6,000 rpm it really came into its own. *AutoExpress/Evo*

GPX/GP-R MIVEC V-6

MITSUBISHI FTO GPX/GP-R MIVEC V-6
SPECIFICATIONS

Weight	2,643 lbs/1,199 kg	0–60 mph	6.7 sec
Layout	FE V-6 NA FWD	0–100 mph	n/a
Displacement	2.0 liters	Top speed	138 mph
Max power	197 bhp @ 7500 rpm	Years in production	1994–2000
Max torque	147 lb/ft @ 6000 rpm	Cost in Gran Turismo	
Transmission	5-speed manual	credits	21,600

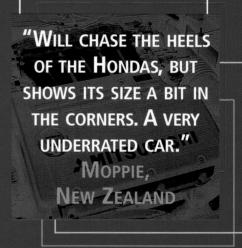

"WILL CHASE THE HEELS OF THE HONDAS, BUT SHOWS ITS SIZE A BIT IN THE CORNERS. A VERY UNDERRATED CAR."
MOPPIE,
NEW ZEALAND

Besides dramatic looks, the FTO was also among the best balanced front drivers of its time, with very neutral handling characteristics. *AutoExpress/Evo*

Styling is perhaps the most subjective aspect of the FTO. Covered headlights, a big grille opening, and fairly long rear deck give this coupe a look unlike any other. *AutoExpress/Evo*

collectible lightweight MIVEC GP-R. Though the little FTO is still one of the best performance bargains out there and is rapidly gaining a following, it remains one of Japan's best-kept automotive secrets.

Sporty and fun to drive, the S13 came in several different guises: Silvia coupe/180 and 200 SX fastbacks, plus the North America-only 240 SX coupe and hatchback. This Silvia features fixed headlights; the others had pop-up units. *John Russell*

Although it's now starting to gain enthusiast popularity in Europe and the United States, the S13 Nissan Silvia/SX has been one of Japan's favorite performance cars for years. Introduced in May 1988 as a replacement for its "shaped like the box it came in" S12 predecessor, the S13 was initially offered in two-door notchback form (Silvia) with a 1.8-liter DOHC four-cylinder power plant (increased to 2.0 liters in 1991) in either naturally aspirated or turbocharged form and a choice of five-speed manual or three-speed automatic overdrive transmissions. Boasting a solid rear-drive chassis with all-independent suspension and offered in three trim levels—J's, Q's, and K's (as in Jack, Queen, and King)—it was joined a few months later by a slinky two-door coupe/hatchback called 180 SX.

The SX was mechanically similar but featured pop-up headlights and the 1.8-liter turbocharged four as standard, boasting 200 bhp. Europeans got the 180, called the 200 SX, while Nissan installed a bigger 2.4-liter normally aspirated four-cylinder for the U.S. and Canada, resulting in the 240 SX. The 240 SX was offered in both hatchback and notchback forms—the latter essentially a Silvia body with a 180 front clip. A special version of the 240 SX notchback was also built, with right-hand drive, for Japan and the Far East.

Just as the 5.0-liter Mustang became a hit in the United States during the 1990s, so did the S13 180 SX/Silvia in Japan. It was affordable, fast, relatively easy to tune, and its rear-drive handling characteristics made it a favorite on both street and track. It was especially popular for drifting, a competition where drivers see who can maintain oversteer (and hence a tail-out drift) for the longest possible time while going through corners. The S13 became the undisputed drifting king. In fact, S13s become so popular for drifting duty that Nissan released a special "drifting" JDM hybrid version, called the SilEighty (a 180 SX with some unique parts and a Silvia nose).

Although superseded by the bigger and more refined S14 in

The 1.8- and 2.0-liter engines found in these cars are strong, durable power plants and, as Japanese tuners discovered, excellent candidates for hot rodding. Factory rated at around 200 bhp, many tuners were able to coax out well over 300 bhp. *John Russell*

240 SX/SILVIA

NISSAN 180/200/240 SX/SILVIA
SPECIFICATIONS

Weight	2,579 lbs/1,170 kg	0–60 mph	6.2 sec
Layout	FE I-4T RWD	0–100 mph	n/a
Displacement	2.0 liters	Top speed	138 mph
Max power	202 bhp @ 6000 rpm	Years in production	1991–94
Max torque	200 lb/ft @ 4400 rpm	Cost in Gran Turismo	
Transmission	5-speed manual	credits	20,360

"YEE HA! MAKES FOR A GREAT DRIFT CAR, JUST LIKE IN REAL LIFE."
MOPPIE,
NEW ZEALAND

In Europe, the S13 fastback far outsold the notchback coupe. Although it packed a 1.8-liter turbocharged four and a choice of five-speed manual or three-speed automatic gearboxes, the car was labeled a 200 SX in these markets. *AutoExpress/Evo*

A good chassis and excellent suspension made the S13 Silvia/ SX a favorite with sports car enthusiasts and "drifters" in Japan. Even today, these cars boast one of the largest aftermarket followings in their home country. *John Russell*

1994, the older car remained very popular and continued in production for several more years in Japan. Although the newer S14 was clearly more sophisticated, it lacked the light weight, agility, and raw performance that made its predecessor such fun to drive. Today, many enthusiasts in the Western Hemisphere are taking cues from their Japanese counterparts, building their own S13 Silvia derivatives by combining their export market cars with off-the-shelf Japanese home-market parts.

This was perhaps one of the most surprising vehicles to come from General Motors' European operations. Eyeing the tremendous success of the Lotus Elise, GM figured it would be a great idea to tailor the package for its mainstream Opel (Continental Europe) and Vauxhall (U.K.) brands and market it as an image and sales booster.

They started with a lightweight bonded-aluminum chassis and all-around double wishbone independent suspension designed by Lotus, dropped in a 147 bhp, 2.2 liter, 16-valve DOHC Ecotec four-cylinder engine, a five-speed close ratio manual gearbox, and wrapped the whole package in a fiber-reinforced body that boasted some of the slinkiest and most distinctive open-cockpit styling ever seen.

Although clearly derived from the Lotus Elise, the Speedster/VX 220 differs in many ways. Styling is more dramatic and utterly unique. In Britain, the car wore Vauxhall badging. Elsewhere in Europe, it was an Opel. *AutoExpress/Evo*

Built at Lotus' facility in Hethel, Norfolk, sitting on tasty 16-inch wheels with ultra low-profile rubber, and featuring massive 280-mm diameter brakes, the Speedster/VX220 is a true dual-purpose road/race car in the traditional sense—it even features a Momo steering wheel, dash-mounted starter button, and a refreshing lack of creature comforts in its wonderfully styled interior.

Although 147 bhp may not be much in early twenty-first century terms, this car really pays homage to its Lotus roots, being ultra light (approximately 1,941 lbs./880 kg), which results in an excellent power-to-weight ratio of 166 bhp per ton. Not surprisingly, it's extremely quick: 0 to 60 in 5.6 seconds and top speeds close to 140 mph are the

The interior has everything you need—full instrumentation, sport steering wheel, and figure-hugging buckets—and nothing you don't—no climate control, DVD player, or jumbo cup holders. *AutoExpress/Evo*

VAUXHALL VX220

OPEL SPEEDSTER/VAUXHALL VX220
SPECIFICATIONS

Weight	1,929 lbs/875 kg	0–60 mph	5.6 sec
Layout	ME I-4 NA RWD	0–100 mph	n/a
Displacement	2.2 liters	Top speed	136 mph
Max power	147 bhp @ 5800 rpm	Years in production	2000–
Max torque	150 lb/ft @ 4000 rpm	Cost in Gran Turismo credits	38,390
Transmission	5-speed manual		

> "IN SIM MODE, THE SPEEDSTER IS A BEAST. I ALWAYS CALL IT THE SMALL [TVR] SPEED 12. GREAT CAR."
> JMR, GERMANY

A total of 147 bhp and a curb weight of under 2,000 lbs (907 kg) translates into excellent acceleration—0 to 60 mph in 5.6 seconds. Lotus patriarch Colin Chapman would no doubt approve.
AutoExpress/Evo

Bumper-mounted exhaust and flying buttress C-pillars give a racy and distinctive look. Not a true convertible but a targa, the Speedster/VX220 also offered a surprisingly snug-fitting roof panel.
AutoExpress/Evo

norm. As for handling ... let's just say it is just about the closest thing to a single-seat race car that the average person can buy. With prices at around £24,000 in Europe brand new, the Speedster/VX220 is an absolute steal!

When it was launched amid "Bug" mania in 1998, the New Beetle wasn't much like its ancestor, being built on a Golf platform and featuring a water-cooled, in-line four-cylinder engine and front-wheel drive. A pleasant and capable car in its own right, it wasn't long before the public began clamoring for a more powerful version.

The first response was the 1.8T, released in early 1999, but more exciting things were in the works. That same year at the Detroit auto show, VW showed a muscular New Beetle concept dubbed "RSI." Inspired by the cars featured in the one-make Beetle Cup series in Germany, the concept incorporated over-the-top styling with a massive bi-level rear wing and huge front air dam, plus a monster exhaust system and 18-inch wheels at all four corners. Under the hood was a twin-turbo V-6 mated to VW's 4motion/Syncro all-wheel drive system. Mouths watered.

The following year at the Geneva Auto Salon, a revised RSI was displayed. It was more

Inspired by the success of the Beetle Cup Racers, the RSI was the ultimate New Beetle. With aggressive styling, torquey V-6 and all-wheel drive, it proved there was more to this little car than dash-mounted vases and pretty colors. *AutoExpress/Evo*

refined and production-like, boasting a body 80 mm wider than the standard Bug thanks to bigger fenders, which were smoothly integrated into the big front air dam, rocker panel extensions, and a rear bumper skirt. At the front, three big grille openings provided unobstructed airflow to the engine. The rear featured cutouts to clear dual tailpipes.

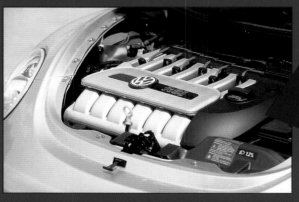

Believe it or not, the 3.2-liter V-6 engine was actually a showcase used in the then-upcoming VW SUV, the Touareg. In New Beetle RSI form, it cranked out 225 bhp at 6,200 rpm. *AutoExpress/Evo*

Other goodies on the 2000 version included an interior with a full complement of gauges, dash-mounted starter button, standard Alcantara upholstery, and a remotely activated in-car entertainment system.

The drivetrain consisted of a new variation of VW's 2.8-liter V-6, bored out to 3.2 liters with four valves per cylinder and dual overhead cams. It cranked out a mighty 225 bhp and was mated to a six-speed manual gearbox, which transmitted power to all four 18-inch wheels via VW's 4motion, full-time all-wheel drive system. The RSI also featured ABS and disc brakes at all four corners.

In 2001, the first RSI models rolled off the line. Ironic considering the New Beetle was largely built in Mexico and

NEW BEETLE RSI

VOLKSWAGEN NEW BEETLE RSI
SPECIFICATIONS

Weight	2,549 lbs/1,156 kg	0–60 mph	5.8 sec
Layout	FE V-6 NA AWD	0–100 mph	n/a
Displacement	3.2 liters	Top speed	140 mph
Max power	225 bhp @ 6200 rpm	Years in production	2001
Max torque	276 lb/ft @ 3200 rpm	Cost in Gran Turismo credits	70,000
Transmission	6-speed manual		

"DOESN'T HANDLE QUITE AS WELL AS IT SHOULD, BUT PLENTY OF GRUNT. THE ENGINE SOUND IS TRULY AMAZING!!"
IY, CANADA

introduced first in the U.S., the RSI version was built strictly for the Continental European market, with the bulk of production going to Germany. VW cited the car's high price, low production run (around 250 in total were built), and prohibitive cost in type approval for not making the car available to North American or Far Eastern buyers.

All 250 RSI models were built to essentially German specification and featured left-hand drive, though a few select cars like this one made their way to other European countries. *AutoExpress/Evo*

From a standing start it could blast to 60 mph in under 6 seconds and top speed was around 140 mph. Handling and grip were also outstanding. For Europeans who wanted a serious performing New Beetle with styling to match, the limited production RSI was the answer to their prayers.

Due to its rarity and exclusivity, few souls were lucky enough to ever witness the car's dramatic styling and performance in the flesh—but for those who did, the RSI left a lasting impression. *AutoExpress/Evo*

CHEVROLET

Since its introduction as a 1967 model, the Camaro, particularly in its sporty SS and Z28 versions, has gained a reputation as an undisputed bang-for-the-buck king. Through the ages, the Camaro remained true to its muscle car roots, relying on a simple but very effective formula of a big-inch pushrod V-8 and a rear-drive, live-axle chassis.

The SS was discontinued in 1972, but for 1996 the nameplate was revived again as a limited edition option on the swoopy fourth-generation Camaro. SS equipment included an SLP (Street Legal Performance) cold-air induction kit, specifically tuned exhaust and suspension, a six-speed Borg Warner transmission with Hurst shifter, unique 17-inch wheels, and a scooped hood.

With 305 bhp and tremendous torque coming from its rumbling 5.7-liter pushrod LT1 V-8, it became a favorite in stoplight Grands Prix on the street and at the drag strip during the 1990s, where few cars could touch it. It was a competent handler too, capable of mixing it up with cars costing more than twice as much.

In 1998, it received new front-end styling and GM's all-new 5.7-liter LS1 engine (still with pushrods and two valves per cylinder), which bumped power to 325 bhp.

Despite offering possibly the best power-per-dollar ratio on the planet, the mighty Camaro SS

Fourth-generation SS Camaros were distinguished from lesser Z28s by a unique hood with central "mail slot," scoop, special 17-inch wheels, SS emblems, and different outlets for the exhaust. *Jerry Heasley*

remained underappreciated by the masses. Sadly, GM decided to phase out production in 2002. The last SS Camaros were offered with special red paint and silver stripes as part of a thirty-fifth anniversary package.

Although the Camaro is gone, it certainly isn't forgotten. Rumors abound that Chevy is working on a successor, true to the spirit of the original and best GM ponycar.

Despite having a smaller displacement, the 5.7-liter pushrod V-8 in the "new" SS was far more efficient than its hallowed big-block ancestor and acceleration was equal too, if not better. *Jerry Heasley*

CAMARO SS

CHEVROLET CAMARO SS
SPECIFICATIONS

Weight	3,411 lbs/1,547 kg	0–60 mph	5.2 sec
Layout	FE V-8 NA RWD	0–100 mph	n/a
Displacement	5.7 liters	Top speed	160 mph (est.)
Max power	325 bhp @ 5200 rpm	Years in production	1995–2002
Max torque	350 lb/ft @ 4000 rpm	Cost in Gran Turismo	
Transmission	6-speed manual	credits	29,530

"Surprised me in how well it handles. A lot of car, but very quick."
Moppie, New Zealand

Truth be told, the SS wasn't a model in its own right but an option package on the Camaro Z28. SLP converted regular Z28s into SS models at its facility near Montreal before shipping them to dealers. *Jerry Heasley*

Swoopy fourth-generation Camaro styling incorporated composite plastic body panels. The windshield had a rake of 68 degrees, which at the time was among the steepest angles seen on a volume production sports coupe. *Jerry Heasley*

CHEVROLET

America's favorite sports car has been a description synonymous with the Chevy Corvette for many years, though for 2001, the label became more relevant than ever. Even though GM had made attempts at creating a Ferrari killer before (including the 1990–95 ZR1), the reborn Z06 was a U.S.-made sports car that really could take on the greatest supercars of Europe and win, and at a fraction of the price.

The Z06 (the name was originally used for competition versions of the 1963 Sting Ray) was introduced for 2001. Using the lighter hardtop body, engineers installed a fortified version of the LS1 5.7-liter V-8 (dubbed LS6, which cranked out 385 bhp), tuned the suspension and chassis, and fitted bigger brakes, along with 18-inch wheels and sticky Goodyear F1 tires. For 2002 they fiddled with LS6's intake and exhaust, resulting in a power hike to an impressive 405 bhp.

In nearly every test conducted by the automotive press, the Z06 out-accelerated, out-cornered, and out-braked some of the most revered cars in the world, including Ferrari's 360 Modena and Porsche's 911 Turbo. Furthermore, it achieved this giant-killing ability without sacrificing anything in the way of creature comforts. You could fly down the back straight of your favorite circuit at 155 mph and pull more than 0.95 lateral g through the corners, all while

Taking its name from a road racing option package on the 1963 Sting Ray, the Z06 was a real performance bargain. Its understated looks hid a firebreathing muscle monster. *Jerry Heasley*

To some eyes, the interior was perhaps a tad bland, but it was comfortable, ergonomically sound, and boasted one of the best audio and climate control systems yet found in a factory sports car. *Jerry Heasley*

CORVETTE Z06

CHEVROLET CORVETTE Z06
SPECIFICATIONS

Weight	3,115 lbs/1,413 kg	0–60 mph	4.0 sec
Layout	FE V-8 NA RWD	0–100 mph	n/a
Displacement	5.7 liters	Top speed	171 mph
Max power	405 bhp @ 6000 rpm	Years in production	2001–
Max torque	400 lb/ft @ 4000 rpm	Cost in Gran Turismo	
Transmission	6-speed manual	credits	54,000

"Big, heavy, and fast. Need to tune carefully to make it work well."
IY, Canada

Although power output on the 2002 Z06 was 405 horses, the same as the old 1993–95 ZR-1, the Z06 was more tractable than its exotic-engined predecessor. *Jerry Heasley*

listening to your favorite CD with the air conditioning on full. With the race over, while other competitors put their race cars on trailers, you could get into your Z06 and drive all the way home, mingling with rush hour traffic on the way—such is the car's civility. Not surprisingly, the Z06 became a favorite with weekend racers and proved highly competitive in Sports Car Club of America-sanctioned events. As time marches on, the Z06 will no doubt enter the annals of history as one of the greatest sports cars the world has ever seen. GM and the United States should be proud.

A rear-mounted transaxle gave the fifth-generation Corvette almost 50/50 weight distribution and was an integral part in the car's impeccable handling. *Jerry Heasley*

LOTUS ESPIRIT

Perhaps one of the most amazing cars of all time is the Lotus Esprit. Originally launched back in 1975, it was still hanging on in the new millennium. Nearly every new variation was a major improvement on the last.

Take the case of the Sport 350. Launched in 1999, this car was conceived in response to Lotus customer views at the London Motor Show in 1997. In the United Kingdom, the widespread introduction of speed cameras and notable increase in traffic enforcement meant that many owners of fast cars were unable to exercise the true potential of their machines on the open road. As a result, club-sponsored track days began gaining in popularity.

Lotus figured, why not create an Esprit built specifically for dual street/track duty? The engineering department at Hethel started with the V-8 engine Esprit (itself first seen in 1996). They removed about 80 kg in weight by manufacturing the body by hand instead of VARI (Vacuum Assisted Resin Injection) as on other Esprits (this alone shaved 20 kg), making extensive use of aluminum and carbon fiber on the massive rear wing, dashboard, console, shifter, and pedals, and they junked the airbags, power windows, air conditioning, and other non-essential items. The Esprit unibody was also stiffened (particularly at the rear) by 40 percent.

In automotive terms, the Lotus Esprit has been around forever. However, the incredible number of years on the market are testament to a sound, original design. AutoExpress/Evo

Scoops, brake calipers, and cam covers were painted blue for a stark contrast to the New Aluminum paint. Inside, the treatment was mirrored with blue inserts for the seats and door panels, plus plenty of aluminum trim. *AutoExpress/Evo*

To the stiff and light structure, Lotus added an uprated suspension, including bigger shocks, special Eibach springs, and a thicker front sway bar. They also replaced the regular Esprit anchors with a set of massive 320-mm AP racing discs with four-piston calipers and Ferodo pads. Wheels were ultra lightweight 18-inch O.Z. alloys wrapped with massive 35-series Michelin Pilot tires.

With an almost mechanically unchanged 3.5-liter V-8 behind the cockpit, the Sport 350 was

SPORT 350

LOTUS ESPIRIT SPORT 350
SPECIFICATIONS

Weight	2,864 lbs/1,299 kg	0–60 mph	4.3 sec
Layout	ME V-8 NA RWD	0–100 mph	9.9 sec
Displacement	3.5 liters	Top speed	175 mph
Max power	350 bhp @ 6500 rpm	Years in production	1999–2000
Max torque	295 lb/ft @ 4250 rpm	Cost in Gran Turismo credits	113,540
Transmission	6-speed manual		

> "LIKE IN REAL LIFE, ONE OF THE MOST UNDERRATED CARS IN GRAN TURISMO. HANDLING IS SIMPLY BRILLIANT!"
> UNKNOWN

The front air dam and massive rear wing were functional. The latter was mainly constructed from carbon fiber with aluminum used for the end panels. *AutoExpress/Evo*

was every bit a true Lotus—albeit the quickest and best yet.

The Sport 350 is wonderfully neutral, and even at the limit doesn't present too much trouble. With a few laps under your belt, it is possible to perform a few quality power slides at low to moderate speeds. Just like the handling, stopping power is out of this world. Even running the car hard lap after lap has virtually no effect on braking ability. The only problem was that just 50 lucky buyers managed to get their hands on a Sport 350. Bummer.

simply the most exhilarating Esprit ever built. A heavy clutch and raw character made it one of the most demanding cars to drive well, but those who mastered the Esprit Sport 350 were rewarded with a driving sensation like no other. Acceleration was fantastic—0 to 60 mph in a blurry shade over 4 seconds. Through the corners (on street or track) it

Weight savings made the Sport almost a second quicker to 60 mph than other Esprits and able to generate plenty of smoke from the huge 295/35ZR18 Michelin Pilot rear tires. *AutoExpress/Evo*

MAZDA RX-7

You have to give Toyo Kogoyo Industries from Hiroshima a great deal of credit. When the German company NSU gave up on Felix Wankel's rotary engine, the Japanese concern bought the rights and persisted, despite the naysayers. The company sorted out reliability problems and coaxed some serious power from the engine. This led to the very interesting Mazda Cosmo Sport and several intriguing rotary-powered coupes and sedans labeled RX (to distinguish them from their piston-engined counterparts).

Ultimately, the car that really put rotary engine technology on the map was the RX-7. Launched for 1978, this little two-seater was an affordable thrill ride that became a hit not only in Japan but around the world. A bigger, more sophisticated RX-7 II (also dubbed Savanna in Japan) arrived on the scene in 1986 and even spawned a convertible version.

Gorgeous styling, race-car-like handling and power aplenty made the FD RX-7 a favorite with enthusiasts and the motoring press, but sadly not with the motoring public. *John Russell*

But it was the third-generation car introduced in 1993 that really turned up the heat. Smooth and sleek combined with a race car–like cockpit and stance, the FD RX-7 III (Efini in Japan) looked like a winner even when parked, but it was the car's performance that made it worthy of entry into the supercar leagues. Packing 255 bhp from its twin-turbocharged, 1.3-liter rotary, the RX-7 outperformed everything in *Motor Trend*'s annual Bang for the Buck contest and also garnered the magazine's prestigious Import Car of the Year award. Enthusiasts and magazine writers fell all over themselves. Mazda had long sought to prove that rotaries could kick the sludge out of piston engines, and with the third-gen RX-7 they finally did. With its great acceleration and superb handling, the RX-7 become a favorite weekend toy and a prominent participant in Japanese sports car racing and N1 Super Touring, as well as SCCA-sanctioned events in the United States.

However, problems soon surfaced. First among them was a tendency for the RX-7's rotary to blow up, which (particularly in the United States) caused Mazda some real headaches with expensive warranty claims.

Displacing just 1.3 liters, the little Rotary cranked out an incredible 255 bhp thanks to twin turbochargers and above average induction and exhaust. It propelled the RX-7 to 5.4-second 0 to 60 mph times and a top speed of over 150 mph. *AutoExpress/Evo*

MAZDA RX-7
SPECIFICATIONS

Weight	2,888 lbs/1,310 kg	0–60 mph	5.4 sec
Layout	FE RTT RWD	0–100 mph	n/a
Displacement	1.3 liters	Top speed	156 mph
Max power	255 bhp @ 6500 rpm	Years in production	1993–95*
Max torque	220 lb/ft @ 5000 rpm	Cost in Gran Turismo credits	37,780
Transmission	5-speed manual		

*JDM production until 2002

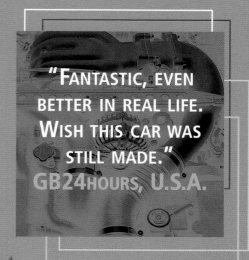

"FANTASTIC, EVEN BETTER IN REAL LIFE. WISH THIS CAR WAS STILL MADE." GB24HOURS, U.S.A.

The cockpit is comfy and snug, and everything is within easy reach. Many people who've driven an RX-7 say you actually wear it rather than sit in it, so in tune is the vehicle with its pilot. *AutoExpress/Evo*

perhaps its biggest publicity boost ever——a tuned version built by Veilside and dubbed the FD 3S Dominator made the RX-7 a major star in the street racing movie *The Fast and the Furious*.

Second, the downturn in the Japanese economy in the 1990s, with a rising yen, made the once affordable sports car decidedly expensive next to home-grown competition in Europe and the United States. Sales suffered, and Mazda decided to pull the plug on export versions in 1995, though the car continued in production for JDM consumption, bowing out in 2002.

Today the RX-7 maintains an enthusiast following around the world. In 2001, the car got

Even today few cars come close to matching the RX-7 in all-around performance, either through numbers or in terms of sheer driving pleasure. *AutoExpress/Evo*

MAZDA RX-8

It takes courage to produce something truly unique in the modern automotive marketplace. Mazda deserves credit for doing just that by producing the RX-8: a fully fledged four-seat, four-door rotary-powered sports car! Perhaps not entirely surprising, this car almost didn't make it. Back in the mid-1990s, Mazda began working on a successor to its third-generation RX-7. However, when Ford took control of the Hiroshima company, plans were put on hold.

Nevertheless, Mazda was determined to show the Blue Oval brass that rotary-powered sports cars did have a future— but with a twist. The result was a concept vehicle called the RX-Evolv, which featured an updated version of the 1.3 rotary engine, room for four adults and four doors, but with

Even before the demise of the RX-7, Mazda was playing with the idea of a next-generation sports car to be powered by a new version of its twin rotary engine dubbed "Renesis." The result, which emerged for 2003, was logically labeled RX-8 but was unique in that it had four doors. *Mazda USA*

coupe-like styling. Mazda displayed it at the 1999 Tokyo Motor Show, where it became the talk of the town. Many doubted whether a four-door, four-seat sports car could succeed, but Mazda pressed ahead regardless.

By 2001 the car (now dubbed RX-8) had undergone some significant styling and engineering tweaks. It boasted very sleek lines (almost a cross between an Alfa Romeo and a Maserati) and incredible interior room thanks to a long, 106.3-inch wheelbase. Under the hood was still the 1.3-liter rotary, similar to that in the old RX-7 but rated at 250 bhp. Teamed with it was a six-speed manual gearbox. The most amazing part of the car, however, was its chassis. With no traditional B pillar behind the front doors, it would seem that body flex would be all too apparent. However, RX-8 engineers put tremendous amounts of extra bracing in the floor.

The result was a superbly balanced combination of acceleration, handling, and braking. In fact, driving the RX-8 could be seen as piloting

From the outside, the RX-8 was faintly reminiscent of an Alfa or Maserati. The rear doors hinged open in suicide fashion, revealing a genuine pair of seats behind the driver and front passenger. *Mazda USA*

MAZDA RX-8
SPECIFICATIONS

Weight	2,970 lbs/1,347 kg	0–60 mph	6.0 sec
Layout	FE R NA RWD	0–100 mph	n/a
Displacement	1.3 liters	Top speed	155 mph (est.)
Max power	250 bhp @ 8500 rpm	Years in production	2003–
Max torque	162 lb/ft @ 7500 rpm	Cost in Gran Turismo	
Transmission	6-speed manual	credits	75,000

"PRETTY QUICK FOR ITS CLASS AND HANDLES WELL. IT WORKS WELL FOR ME ON SHORTER TRACKS AND STREET-TYPE COURSES LIKE TOKYO R246 AND SEATTLE."
UNKNOWN

A significant part of the RX-8's amazingly fun-to-drive nature was the very direct steering and slick six-speed gearbox with ultra-short shifter. *Mazda USA*

a bigger and faster Miata roadster. For all its exotic engineering, Mazda was determined to keep prices competitive. For its North American introduction, prices started under the $30,000 mark. Time will tell if the RX-8 proves successful, but at this point it seems that Mazda has added all the ingredients required to make it a winner.

Early spy shots saw the car wearing massive 20-inch wheels , though production versions came standard with 18-inchers at all four corners. *Mazda USA*

MITSUBISHI LANCER

In a global automotive landscape littered with an ever-growing number of big, heavy, ponderous, gadget-laden mobile conveyances, the Mitsubishi Lancer Evolution VII stands out. It's a good old-fashioned, single-purpose, seat-of-your-pants performance car—a homologation special built without compromise.

This car emerged from very workaday beginnings to clean up in World Championship Rallying. As a result of this and its inclusion in Gran Turismo, the Evo became arguably the most desirable four-door sedan in the world.

When you get behind the wheel of an Evo, just about every other performance car seems utterly pointless and irrelevant. What else will do the grocery store and commuter runs day-in and day-out, be quicker than nearly anything else on real-world roads, yet still provide roomy seating for four?

The Lancer Evo has been around since 1992, but it wasn't until the IV version arrived in 1996 that the world

An utterly crazy car for somber, sensible times, the EVO VII apologized to no one with its outrageous styling and equally insane performance. On a daily basis virtually no other production car was as quick, either in a straight line or through the corners. *John Russell*

began to sit up and take notice. The V and even more outrageous VI turned it into a superstar both on and off the Rally circuit (finally eclipsing the Subaru Impreza), and the VII continues the legacy. Outwardly the Evo VII is subtler, albeit more angular looking, than its immediate predecessors, though don't think for a second that this equates to lesser performance.

Underhood sits essentially the same 2.0 liter turbocharged four rated at a very conservative 276 bhp (for those good ol' Japanese government requirements) and 275 lb-ft of torque. A five-speed manual gearbox, all-wheel drive system with Active Center Differential and Yaw Control, along with massive Brembo brakes, mean essentially one thing—no-holds-barred driving fun.

This car does it all—dragster-style acceleration (one test car was clocked at 0 to 60 mph in 4.4 seconds) and touring-car style handling. Very direct steering and the fantastic suspension and AWD system are combined with glue-like Yokohama Advan tires. The active differential and yaw control kick in once you enter a fast turn, selecting the tightest

Conservatively rated at 276 bhp, the Evo VII's overachieving four-cylinder turbo engine actually makes over 350 horsepower, and with the whole car weighing at just a shade under 3,000 lbs (1,360 kg) you can understand why it is so phenomenally quick. *John Russell*

MITSUBISHI LANCER
EVOLUTION VII GSR/RS SPRINT
SPECIFICATIONS

Weight	2,970 lbs/1,347 kg	0–60 mph	4.4 sec
Layout	FE I-4T AWD	0–100 mph	12.5 sec
Displacement	2.0 liters	Top speed	157 mph
Max power	276 bhp @ 6500 rpm	Years in production	2001–2003
Max torque	282 lb/ft @ 3500 rpm	Cost in Gran Turismo	
Transmission	5-speed manual	credits	25,180

"SHOULD PERHAPS BE A LITTLE QUICKER IN THE GAME. HOWEVER, ONE OF THE FASTEST NON-SPECIFIC RALLY CARS IN THE DIRT." MOPPIE, NEW ZEALAND

Styling of the Lancer Evolution got all muscular with the Evo IV in 1996. The Evo VII toned down the boy racer look, but remained true to its roots, with a gaping hole in the front bumper for the intercooler and massive rear wing. *John Russell*

Pretty, multi-spoke 17-inch wheels provide the necessary clearance for the huge four- and two-piston caliper Brembo brakes. Able to generate ludicrous speeds and lap times, the Evo VII needed every last ounce of stopping power. *John Russell*

line possible. This is a huge factor in the Mitsu's lightning-quick lap times.

So are there any drawbacks to this remarkable rally homologation special? Not really. The interior is bland to some eyes, and the car gets lousy gas mileage for a four-cylinder, but when you get such mind-bending performance for less money than a fully loaded Maxima, these little nitpicks simply pale into insignificance.

NISSAN 300ZX

In terms of sheer numbers, the most successful sports car brand of the last two decades isn't Corvette, Mazda RX-7, or MG, but the Datsun/Nissan Z car series. Prior to the introduction of the fourth-generation Toyota Supra, the Nissan 300ZX was the undisputed King of the Hill when it came to sporty Japanese GTs.

In 1989, Nissan unveiled this iteration of the Z car series, code named Z32. This car was quite a radical departure from its predecessor, with very smooth yet sporty lines and a much-improved interior. Like those that had gone before it, the Z32 adopted the "Fairlady" name in Japan, but elsewhere in the world was simply called 300ZX. Also like previous Z cars, it was offered in either two-seater or 2+2 forms, with a choice of engines and five-speed manual or four-speed automatic transmissions.

No question about it, the Z32 Nissan 300ZX Twin Turbo was one amazing piece of machinery in its day. With 300 bhp and fantastically engineered chassis and suspension, it was a road bound rocket and an absolute hoot to drive. *AutoExpress/Evo*

The new 300ZX was equally impressive under the skin. It boasted one of the stiffest unibody structures yet seen in a sporty car and all-independent multi-link suspension, with four-wheel disc brakes and standard ABS. Under the hood, all versions of the 300ZX utilized Nissan's VG30DETT 3.0-liter V-6 engine in either normally aspirated or turbocharged form. In 222 bhp trim the regular ZX was a fine performing car, but all eyes were naturally on the Twin Turbo version, which delivered an honest 300 bhp (automatic, Japanese, and Euro market cars were rated at 280 bhp) and lightning-quick acceleration. A short wheelbase two-seater Twin Turbo could blast to 60 mph in under 6 seconds flat and top out well in excess of 140 mph.

The 300ZX's handling, cornering, and braking (particularly the Twin Turbo) were truly world-class. Turbo versions featured standard electronic damping and HICAS rear-wheel steering—throw the 300ZXTT into a sharp turn, and the rear wheels would first move out a fraction for sharper turn in and then inward to maintain stability

Inside, the Z32 300ZX was loaded to the gills with just about every option you could think of. Leather upholstery? You got it. Climate Control? Absolutely. Power heated mirrors? What do you think? *AutoExpress/Evo*

TWIN TURBO

NISSAN 300ZX TWIN TURBO
SPECIFICATIONS*

Weight	3,505 lbs/1,590 kg	0–60 mph	6.0 sec
Layout	FE V-6TT RWD	0–100 mph	n/a
Displacement	3.0 liters	Top speed	156 mph
Max power	300 bhp @ 6400 rpm	Years in production	1989–2000
Max torque	283 lb/ft @ 3600 rpm	Cost in Gran Turismo	
Transmission	5-speed manual	credits	43,980

* refers to Japanese spec 2+2

"I LOVE THIS CAR. MEGA POWER, MEGA HANDLING. IN MY OPINION, ONE OF THE BEST ALL-AROUND GT MACHINES IN THE GAME."
JESSE B, CANADA

In the United States, the Z32 was sold from 1990 through 1996 in both two-seat and 2+2 versions. In other parts of the world—notably Europe—only the latter was available. Genuine European spec 2+2s are among the rarest of all. *AutoExpress/Evo*

midway through the corner. This, combined with a limited-slip rear differential and ultra sticky rubber, resulted in an exceedingly quick machine around the road course.

Like most Japanese "super sports" cars of the early 1990s, however, the 300ZX was arguably too good (and too expensive). The 300ZX was discontinued from European markets in 1994, and, despite the arrival of the special 365 bhp SMZ version the following year, it went away from arguably its biggest audience, the United States, in 1996. The Z32 remained in production, mainly for the Japanese domestic

market, finally bowing out in 2000 after receiving a handsome facelift. Although now superseded by the 350Z, the older Z32 model maintains a following around the globe.

Such was the performance of the Twin Turbo that magazines and enthusiasts raved. However, its performance wasn't enough to prevent a steady decline in sales that resulted in Americans bidding farewell in 1996. *AutoExpress/Evo*

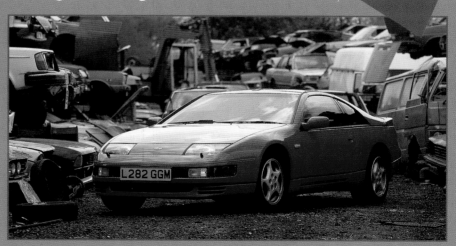

If ever a great sports coupe had truly humble origins, it is the Nissan Skyline, specifically the all-wheel drive R32/33/34 GT-R version. The Skyline has long been one of Japan's most popular family cars since its debut in 1966. The GT-R emblem first appeared on Skylines in 1969 and Nissan resurrected it for a top-shelf version of its new 1989 R32 Skyline. The GT-R (available in base and V-spec versions—the latter fitted with massive Brembo brakes, among other things) featured a 2.6-liter in-line six-cylinder engine with twin turbochargers, a Getrag five-speed manual gearbox, intelligent torque splitting all-wheel drive, and four-wheel steering. Rated at a conservative 280 bhp (the maximum permitted by Japanese law), the GT-R was an absolute road rocket (how does 0 to 60 in 5.7 seconds, quarter mile times in the 13s, and a top speed of 150 mph sound?). Thanks to its all-wheel drive system, it was also ruthlessly efficient and a superb track car. Best of all, it cost the equivalent of around $30,000, which made it one of the best performance car buys anywhere.

Japan had its own true Godzilla in the shape of the Nissan Skyline GT-R. Purists of European machinery gasped in horror as it devoured their beloved sports cars with the same ease as the fabled monster did Tokyo and New York. *AutoExpress/Evo*

The Skyline soon dominated Japan's Group A, N1, and Touring Car series.

In 1995, an improved Skyline (the R33) was launched, based on the Laurel midsize sedan, which meant slightly bigger dimensions and an increase in weight (40 kg). The R33 GT-R was quicker around the track than its predecessor, however, and like the R32, it made a serious impact in Japan's N1 production class race series, outperforming more exotic machinery. It even took the battle to the European's home turf. Nissan U.K. began officially importing R33 GT-Rs, and one car set the lap record on Germany's infamous Nürburgring—in an amazing 8 minutes flat.

Nissan turned up the heat again late in 1998, releasing a revised R34 Skyline lineup with more aggressive styling—particularly at the front. Soon a new GT-R (offered in base and V-spec versions) arrived with front and rear undertrays and a prominent deck spoiler, slightly altered suspension, plus a 2.6-liter straight six engine tuned for more low-end torque and a new Getrag six-speed gearbox. The uplevel V-spec added more aggressive aero body extensions and a more

All Skyline GT-Rs of this vintage came in right-hand drive form only. The 1999-and-up R34 version (seen here) featured a slightly more sporting instrument panel and steering wheel, plus a standard LCD display in the center of the dash. *AutoExpress/Evo*

GT-R V-SPEC

NISSAN SKYLINE GT-R V-SPEC
SPECIFICATIONS*

Weight	2,970 lbs/1,347 kg	0–60 mph	4.7 sec
Layout	FE I-6TT AWD	0–100 mph	12.5 sec
Displacement	2.6 liters	Top speed	165 mph
Max power	280 bhp @ 7000 rpm	Years in production	1999–2002
Max torque	289 lb/ft @ 4400 rpm	Cost in Gran Turismo credits	
Transmission	6-speed manual		55,980

* refers to R34 version

"NOT THE BEAST IT WAS IN GT2. AND THAT CAN BE A GOOD THING."
GB24HOURS, U.S.A.

For most people, the name GT-R evokes images of this car, the R34, though the badge originally belonged on Skylines of the late 1960s. They were just as successful in the touring car circuit then too! *AutoExpress/Evo*

Driving an R32, R33, or R34 GT-R is like nothing else. Acceleration is ear popping and the car's handling, poise, and grip are almost beyond comprehension. *AutoExpress/Evo*

intelligent ATTESSA AWD system. The result was a quicker car—in fact, an R34 beat the previous record set by the R33 on the Nürburgring—posting a time of 7 min 52 sec! Production of R34s ceased in 2002, with the final thousand being Nür-Spec (as in Nürburgring) limited editions, which rapidly sold out. At the time of this writing, plans were in the works for a new Skyline—to be spun off the same versatile FM platform as the 350Z and U.S.-market Infiniti G35.

NISSAN 350Z

Sometimes a car comes along that is so right it changes the status quo. In 1969, the Datsun Fairlady (the Japanese market name for the Z car series) 240Z was that car. Prior to its introduction, sports cars were conceived as contraptions that offered brilliant balance and handling but poor ride, quality control, and reliability—factors that kept them very much at the fringe of the automotive marketplace. The 240Z was faster and handled just as well as some of these offerings, yet boasted greater refinement, reliability, and workmanship.

Not surprisingly, it sold like hot cakes. However, the 240 piled on weight and complexity over time—culminating in the 1990–2000 Fairlady 300ZX, which was a great car but sold poorly.

A revitalized Nissan sought to rectify the problem by introducing the 350Z in 2002 as an 2003 model. With space-age but unmistakably Z-car styling, this two-seat 104.3-inch wheelbase coupe had all the right ingredients to make it a hit: an all-aluminum DOHC 24-valve, 287 bhp V-6, close ratio six-speed manual gearbox, ultra-stiff chassis with four-wheel independent suspension, and a cabin with almost spot-on ergonomics.

Much like the original Z, the new 350 made a huge splash on its debut. Not only was it stunning to behold, it had equally good performance to back up the looks. Even the

Loyalists of the Datsun/Nissan Z are among the most particular of all car enthusiasts, and every time Nissan launches a new one, it faces a tough task improving upon the previous model. In 2002, the all-new Z did just that. *John Russell*

With each evolution of the Z family, the engine seems to grow in size and the 2003 version was no exception. Displacing 3.5 liters and featuring CVTCS (Continuously Variable Timing Control System), it cranks out 287 bhp. *John Russell*

ever-jaded press could not fail to be utterly impressed by its road and track manners. In acceleration, the Z will do the 0 to 60 mph run in about 5.6 seconds and the quarter mile in 14.2 at nearly 100 mph, helped by spades of mid-range torque from the creamy V-6.

Boasting excellent weight distribution—helped by an engine set aft of the front wheels and

(Z CONCEPT)

NISSAN 350Z (Z CONCEPT)
SPECIFICATIONS

Weight	3,290 lbs/1,492 kg	0–60 mph	5.6 sec
Layout	FE V-6 NA RWD	0–100 mph	14.2 sec
Displacement	3.5 liters	Top speed	155 mph (est.)
Max power	287 bhp @ 6200 rpm	Years in production	2002–
Max torque	274 lb/ft @ 4800 rpm	Cost in Gran Turismo	
Transmission	6-speed manual	credits	75,000

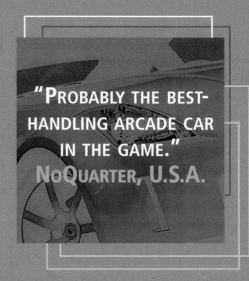

"PROBABLY THE BEST-HANDLING ARCADE CAR IN THE GAME."
NoQUARTER, U.S.A.

A neat feature inside is the fact that the instrument panel adjusts with the tilt steering wheel . Both the main and auxiliary gauge clusters take their inspiration from those in the very first 240 Z. *John Russell*

and weaknesses, the 350Z simply does everything well. Z enthusiasts had very high hopes for this car, and it was nice to see that Nissan paid attention, giving them a vehicle that exceeded their expectations.

lightweight double wishbone suspension mated to the car's tight frame (the Z begs to be flogged around the corners)—it has excellent poise, balance, and grip (especially with the 17- or 18-inch rubber) and will pull almost 0.90 lateral g in the turns. The car's agility and surefoot-edness, even in entry-level form, is truly a credit to its design and engineering. Braking is also excellent. The big ABS assisted discs bite in hard and will bring the 350Z to a complete rest in 113 ft time and again. Track models come standard with meatier Brembo anchors.

Whereas many performance cars in the same price range have easily identifiable strengths

Striking looks were the work of talented designer Ajay Panchal and successfully blended elements of the original 1969 Z with decidedly futuristic overtones. *John Russell*

TOYOTA SUPRA

A great rival to the illustrious Z car since its introduction in 1979, the Supra finally matured into a serious supercar killer with its fourth redesign. One magazine went so far as to label it "Japan's Porsche 928," and in many respects this statement isn't too far from the truth.

Debuting as a 1993 model, this latest Supra marked a radical departure from its predecessor. Here was a big and wide sports coupe with smooth, hunkered-down styling and a choice of true hardtop or targa roof configurations, plus a 3.0-liter straight-six power plant—offered in either normally aspirated (220 bhp) or twin turbocharged (315 bhp) form, with a six-speed manual or four-speed automatic gearbox.

Not surprisingly it was the turbo model that drew the most attention. Although the previous Supra Turbo had been a fairly quick (albeit luxurious) grand tourer, its successor took performance to an entirely new level. Not only was it fast in a straight line, but for such a heavy car (3,450 lbs/1,565 kg) it handled brilliantly (0.98 lateral g), and stopping power was also astonishing—thanks to 12.6-inch diameter disc brakes at all four corners. Buff book writers and enthusiasts alike were amazed (and ecstatic) at the car's performance. It was quicker than a contemporary Corvette or Honda NSX (0 to 60 mph in 5.0 sec) and could hunt

Toyota's grand tourer finally came of age in 1993. Twin turbos, six-speed gearbox, and massive rear wing were the ultimate in Supra style and power. Production lasted from 1993 through 2000. *Jerry Heasley*

down and destroy much more "exotic" supercars.

So good was the basic formula that Toyota wisely didn't change the car much throughout its entire production run. Even as other sport coupes became faster and better handling, the Supra remained the benchmark by which others were judged. However, it was always expensive (it cost around $40,000 in 1993), and the lofty price meant that sales were

marginal at best. When the Japanese economy took a downturn in the mid-1990s, importing the Supra to American and European shores became an non-viable economic option for Toyota. The car was discontinued from these markets in 1996 and 1998, respectively.

This was a great shame, for not only was the Supra a great car in stock trim, but Japanese tuners discovered that both the Supra's chassis and engine

Quad circular taillight lenses were a fourth-generation Supra trademark, and with an all-conquering 3.0-liter twin cam straight six under the hood, those lenses were about all challengers would see once a Supra driver put the pedal to the metal. *Jerry Heasley*

TWIN TURBO (RZ)

TOYOTA SUPRA TWIN TURBO (RZ)
SPECIFICATIONS*

Weight	3,450 lbs/1,565 kg	0–60 mph	5.0 sec
Layout	FE I-6TT RWD	0–100 mph	n/a
Displacement	3.0 liters	Top speed	157 mph
Max power	320 bhp @ 5800 rpm	Years in production	1993–98**
Max torque	315 lb/ft @ 4000 rpm	Cost in Gran Turismo	
Transmission	6-speed manual	credits	44,800

*refers to U.S. specification   ** production until 2000 for JDM

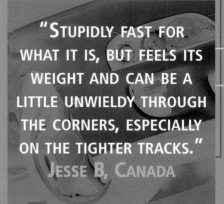

"STUPIDLY FAST FOR WHAT IT IS, BUT FEELS ITS WEIGHT AND CAN BE A LITTLE UNWIELDY THROUGH THE CORNERS, ESPECIALLY ON THE TIGHTER TRACKS."
JESSE B, CANADA

Even today, getting behind the wheel of a Supra Twin Turbo remains a mind-blowing experience. It is also easy to make the already fast Toyota much quicker still, thanks to burgeoning performance aftermarket support. *Jerry Heasley*

Fourth-generation Supras were sold in both turbocharged and normally aspirated forms with either a true hardtop or removable "aero roof." Most European spec cars were the former, with most American and Japanese cars being the latter. *Jerry Heasley*

could handle well in excess of 800 horsepower. These Toyotas became a favorite among the late-night street-racing crowd. Today the Supra Twin Turbo is still an excellent car. Its styling has aged well, its performance remains exhilarating, and although it continues to be a fairly rare sight (particularly on Western roads), a ready aftermarket and growing enthusiast following will ensure its status as a future collectible.

TVR TUSCAN

In this day and age, virtually every car is built with some serious compromises. In most cases, a manufacturer's accounting department prevents the most exotic race-inspired technology from reaching the street. The TVR Tuscan Speed Six is a rare breed in that its form and function weren't dictated by bean counters and brand-management types, but rather by passionate engineers who simply love cars.

The second in a new generation of ultra-high performance TVRs to emerge from this independent British sports car builder, the Tuscan has been a sellout success since its introduction in 2000. It even starred in the Hollywood blockbuster *Swordfish*. And why not? It's a handcrafted, stunningly beautiful two-seat targa coupe with a sumptuous interior, fantastic-sounding straight-six DOHC engine, unforgettable performance, and an air of civility not found in previous TVRs.

Key ingredients in the design and execution of the Tuscan were light weight (a maximum weight of 1,000 kg) and the fact that the car would use the company's new straight-six 3.6 engine. The six may not have seemed an obvious choice, given that most recent TVRs up to that time, including the Griffith, Chimera, and Cerbera, had either come standard with or offered a V-8. The six was chosen because it gave the engineers a lot more

Under the direction of Peter Wheeler, TVR has gone from strength to strength. The Tuscan was conceived for a slightly more mainstream audience than many of the Blackpool sports car builder's previous offerings. *AutoExpress/Evo*

Give the Tuscan a little gas on an open stretch of tarmac, and it will launch down the road in a manner akin to an F-18 taking off a carrier. The powerband is more steady and progressive through the RPM range than V-8-engined TVRs. *AutoExpress/Evo*

options when it came to interior and chassis configuration, and exhaust and emissions. Aside from practical reasons, a straight-six represents a return to British sports car tradition of the old six-powered Jaguars and Astons of the 1950s and 1960s.

Offered in base 3.6 (350 bhp) and Tuscan S 4.0 (390 bhp) versions, the Tuscan is a truly phenomenal road car.

Considering it costs around £40,000 new, it offers unbelievable levels of performance. The 3.6-engined car will accelerate just as quickly as Aston Martin's hallowed Vanquish and reach nearly 170 mph. The S version is quicker still: 0 to 60 in 4.0 sec and 190-plus mph.

And the handling—as you'd expect from a car of this lineage and pedigree—is just

SPEED SIX

TVR TUSCAN SPEED SIX
SPECIFICATIONS*

Weight	2,425 lbs/1,100 kg	0–60 mph	4.0 sec
Layout	FE I-6 NA RWD	0–100 mph	9.3 sec
Displacement	4.0 liters	Top speed	190 mph (est.)
Max power	390 bhp @ 7000 rpm	Years in production	2001–
Max torque	310 lb/ft @ 5250 rpm	Cost in Gran Turismo credits	80,750
Transmission	6-speed manual		

* refers to the Tuscan S

> "DROOOL. NICE CAR, WELL-BALANCED, BUT REQUIRES A GENTLE TOUCH ON THE THROTTLE. WORKS BEST ON THE SMOOTH, FAST CIRCUITS."
> MOPPIE, NEW ZEALAND

as dramatic. Tuscans have been used in a one-make British racing series for more than a decade, with spectacular results. The experience and development work from the competition front really translates well to the street.

The ride is perhaps the most surprising aspect of this car. Normally you would associate such astronomical levels of handling and grip with a harsh ride, but the Tuscan is supple—almost soft—thanks to some very clever suspension tweaking (particularly shock valving). This means that you can drive the car long distances and not feel tired and sore after the first hour. How many 170-mph supercars can boast that for a similar price?

Besides looks and performance, a wonderful exhaust note is a hallmark of TVRs. The Tuscan emits an authoritative rumble somewhat reminiscent of a classic XK-engined Jaguar and distinctly different from a V-8 car. *AutoExpress/Evo*

Like nearly every TVR built since the mid-1990s, styling of the Tuscan is muscular, beautiful, and utterly unique. Originally conceived to be a true convertible, strength and safety issues ultimately resulted in a targa configuration being adopted. *AutoExpress/Evo*

CHEVROLET

Even before the fifth-generation Corvette was introduced for public consumption, Chevy knew that it wanted to take the car racing—and not just any type of racing. Specifically, it wanted to take on Europe's big guns and Chrysler's Viper in the legendary 24 hours of Le Mans and other endurance races.

For this task, Chevy contracted Pratt & Miller to build a factory race car using the regular, street-going C5 as the starting point. The basic steel backbone chassis was retained, though stretched to 104.7 inches, and the suspension was tweaked with different lower front A arms and upper control arms at the back. Multi-adjustable coil-over shocks were substituted for the transverse leaf spring at the front. Amazingly, the rest of the car remain essentially stock C5 underneath. Massive Alcon lightweight brakes and heavy-duty spindles were also installed.

As for the engine and drivetrain, the C5-R has a special 6.0-liter V-8 under the hood, which incorporates dry sump oiling and a racing fuel injection system. Compared to the stock Vette's 345 bhp, the race motor cranks out a whopping 620 horses. The transmission is a five-speed manual mounted directly ahead of the rear axle for optimum weight distribution (just like a regular C5). The elongated body is made from carbon fiber, and the car rides on massive

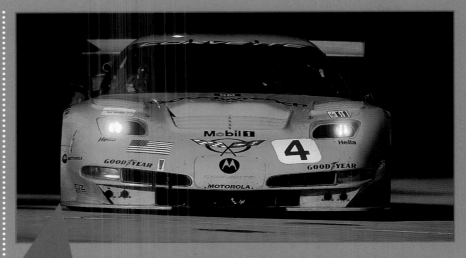

Corvettes have entered road racing in all shapes and forms over the years, but one of the most successful has been the distinctive yellow Pratt & Miller C5-Rs that dominated sports car and endurance racing in the GTS class. *Richard Prince*

18-inch BBS wheels and ultra sticky race rubber. Total weight is nearly 1,000 lbs (454 kg) less than a regular C5, which can mean only one thing—earth-shattering acceleration, cornering, and braking. It's a pity Chevy didn't go through with a street version, as it would have blown everything else into the weeds.

The C5-R was first unveiled in 1999 to a receptive audience at the annual SEMA show in Las Vegas and soon afterward was in competition. Since then it has been onward and upward. The distinctive yellow C5-Rs won overall at the Rolex 24 at Daytona and finished first and second in the GTS class

On its first competition outing at the 2001 Daytona Rolex 24 hours, the yellow C5-R got off to a fantastic start and ultimately emerged victorious, crossing the line to finish first overall. *Richard Prince*

CORVETTE C5-R

CHEVROLET CORVETTE C5-R
SPECIFICATIONS

Weight	2,510 lbs/1,139 kg	0–60 mph	3.8 sec (est.)
Layout	FE V-8 NA RWD	0–100 mph	n/a
Displacement	6.0 liters	Top speed	230 mph (est.)
Max power	620 bhp @ 6400 rpm	Years in production	2000–
Max torque	495 lb/ft @ 5200 rpm	Cost in Gran Turismo	
Transmission	5-speed manual	credits	1,000,000

"AWESOME! ON PAR WITH THE VIPER AS THE FASTEST RACE-SPEC CAR."
MOPPIE, NEW ZEALAND

Originally, a street-going counterpart was required in order for the C5 Corvette to compete in FIA GT racing, but the rules changed leaving plans for a street-version stillborn. Given the C5-Rs success record, imagine what kind of car the street version would have been. *Richard Prince*

After a dominant GTS victory in 2001, the Pratt & Miller racers were back in action at Le Mans for 2002. Although they faced some stiff competition from the Prodrive Ferrari 550, the 'vettes came through to win their class yet again. *Richard Prince*

championship at Le Mans in 2001 and 2002, with Ron Fellows, Oliver Gavin, and Johnny O'Connell taking the checkered flag, followed by teammates Andy Pilgrim, Kelly Collins, and Franck Freon. Like the Vipers before them, the C5-Rs proved a force to be reckoned within FIA GT circles.

DODGE VIPER

Beating the Europeans at Le Mans is a long-standing American dream that simply refuses to die. Back in the 1960s, Ford took on the might of Ferrari with its GT40 and walked all over the competition. Nearly 30 years later, the United States once again became a force to be reckoned with. This time, Chrysler and the Dodge Viper led the assault.

What was perhaps most amazing about the Dodge effort was that the Viper race cars were essentially stock 1996 GTS coupes. The basic chassis, V-10 engine, and styling where retained—though many hours in the wind tunnel resulted in distinctive body extensions and a massive rear wing. Chrysler's engineers fiddled with the monster 8.0-liter V-10 motor, managing to coax an amazing 650 bhp out of it in racing trim.

In accordance with FIA GT rules at the time, Dodge had to build 500 versions for public sale in order for the Viper to compete at Le Mans. A street GTS-R was unveiled at Monterey in 1995, to much acclaim. The street versions quickly sold out and many ended up in the hands of privateer racers, becoming frequent sights at SCCA and other sanctioned events. In their first outing at Le Mans, despite stiff competition and extensive wear and tear, one Viper managed to finish the grueling 24-hour event

When Dodge came out with its Viper GTS coupe, it was perhaps only natural that a racing version should emerge. The resulting GTS-R was unveiled to a warm public reception and soon entered into motorsport competition. *AutoSport/LAT*

Costing a whopping $250,000, most GTS-Rs, not surprisingly, ended up on the SCCA/FIA race circuit and in the hands of privateers. *Dan Carney*

in a very respectable 10th place overall.

Realizing that the car would probably be even more competitive in the production-based GT2 category, Dodge switched its efforts, with outstanding results. In the 1997 FIA GT2 Championship, the works Vipers swept all before them, winning both the constructor's and driver's cups before the end of the season.

With such a great success under their belt, Team Viper prepared for another assault on Le Mans the following year. In practice, a Viper set the fastest lap for GT2. In the race, the distinctive white-and-blue Vipers led their class from the start and dominated throughout the race.

GTS-R

DODGE VIPER GTS-R
SPECIFICATIONS

Weight	2,750 lbs/1,247 kg	0–60 mph	3.2 sec (est.)
Layout	FE V-10 NA RWD	0–100 mph	n/a
Displacement	8.0 liters	Top speed	225 mph
Max power	650 bhp @ 6000 rpm	Years in production	1996–99
Max torque	650 lb/ft @ 5000 rpm	Cost in Gran Turismo credits	n/a
Transmission	6-speed manual		

"DEFINITELY NOT FOR THE FAINT-HEARTED, THIS ONE."
GB24HOURS, U.S.A.

Excellent reliability helped Dodge clinch a 1-2 at Le Mans for two consecutive seasons and win the FIA GT2 championship. *Autosport/LAT*

Although it looked similar to the GTS coupe, the R model incorporated extensive use of carbon fiber for its structure and curb weight was around 2,750 lbs (1,247 kg). A regular street GTS tipped the scales at around 3,500 lbs (1,588 kg). *Dan Carney*

They finished 11th overall, a magnificent 1-2 in GT2. It was a stunning victory for Chrysler, and the first time in 30 years that an American-built automobile had seen the winners' circle at this most prestigious of sports car racing events.

Vipers did it again the following year, cleaning up in GT2 and finishing in five of the top six places in their category, with the Justin Bell/Bobby Archer machine taking the flag for its class. Both Chrysler and the U.S.A. had now proved they were seriously competitive and could beat the Europeans.

A marque with a long history of sports car racing and builder of one of the most powerful supercars in the 1990s, Lister remains little-known outside the arena of die-hard auto enthusiasts. It's quite a shame, really, considering Lister's achievements.

The company can trace its origins back to 1954, when company founder Brian Lister built his first car, which competed against Aston Martin DBs and Jaguar's famous C and D type racers in the British sports car arena. By 1958, Lister was making waves—the debut of the Lister Jaguar led to the starting grid at Le Mans and a win in the support race for the British Grand Prix, with legendary Formula 1 and sports car driver Stirling Moss at the helm.

Not long after, Lister took a protracted retirement from the world of sports cars. It wasn't until the mid-1980s, with a new front man—Laurence Pearce—that the company once again turned its attention to serious automobiles. Using its ties with Jaguar, Lister built the handcrafted, TWR V-12 mid-engined Storm GTL supercar, which went on sale in 1993. An immensely powerful machine (it made over 500 bhp) and boasting an excellent lightweight aluminum chassis, carbon fiber body, and superb suspension and brakes, the company had the perfect weapon with which to re-enter the elite world of GT sports car racing.

Making its return to sports cars after a long absence, Lister Cars, under the direction of Laurence Pearce, unveiled its Storm GTL in 1993. *AutoExpress/Evo*

Sold in limited numbers, the ultra-fast Storm GTL was hand-built to order in Britain. It featured aggressive styling and an enormous 7.0 liter Jaguar-derived V-12 cranking out 594 bhp, thanks to MOTEC electronic management and other tweaks. *AutoExpress/Evo*

A GT1 version of the Storm (complete with 562 bhp 7.0-liter V-12) was thus soon in action at the Le Mans and Daytona 24-hour events, as well as the BPR International GT series. Despite early teething troubles, the Lister Storm GT1 matured into a superb sports racer and was always a serious contender.

Lister finished second overall in the 1998 GT1 season, but it was the

GTL/GT1

LISTER STORM GTL/GT1
SPECIFICATIONS

Weight	3,168 lbs/1,437 kg	0–60 mph	4.1 sec
Layout	ME V-12 NA RWD	0–100 mph	n/a
Displacement	7.0 liters	Top speed	200 mph
Max power	594 bhp @ 6100 rpm	Years in production	1993–
Max torque	580 lb/ft @ 3450 rpm	Cost in Gran Turismo credits	1,198,000
Transmission	6-speed manual		

"INTERESTING CAR. VERY FAST, BUT REQUIRES A CAREFUL AND VERY CONTROLLED DRIVING STYLE."
MOPPIE,
NEW ZEALAND

A version of the GTL was built to compete in the FIA GT Sports Car championship. In 1999, it not only won both classes of the Privilege Insurance GT Championship, but it also competed in four rounds of the FIA GT series—setting the fastest qualifying time twice and finishing second, third, and fourth in three of the four events. *National Motor Museum, Beaulieu*

Independent, four-wheel, double-wishbone suspension was standard on Storm, as was MOTEC data logging equipment and an onboard jacking system. *AutoSport/LAT*

following year that saw the team bask in glory. With Storms running in both the GT1 and GT2 categories of the Privilege Insurance GT Championship, works drivers Julian Bailey, Jamie Campbell-Walker, and David Warnock drove to victory in both classes. Bailey and Campbell-Walker also piloted the Storm to a championship win in the RAC (Royal Automobile Club) Tourist Trophy and Oulton Park Gold Cup, taking the checkered flag in seven of the 11 championship rounds.

MAZDA 787B

Out of all the cars to win the prestigious 24 hours of Le Mans, Mazda's 787B stands out as a true triumph of the determination to succeed. It is also significant in being the only car from a non-American or European manufacturer to triumph at the Sarthe circuit.

To some, the 1991 victory may seem like a fluke, but if we delve a little deeper into Mazda's history, we'll see that it was anything but. Toyo Kogoyo (Mazda's original name) bought the rights to Felix Wankel's flawed rotary engine in 1961 and gradually ironed out the bugs. However, even when shoehorned into the beautiful Mazda Cosmo 110S, public reception of the new engine wasn't exactly enthusiastic.

Mazda decided to build racing versions of the Cosmo and take them to Europe to prove that rotaries were just as good, if not better, than their piston-engine counterparts. This first racing venture was in the grueling 84 (yes 84) hours Marathon de La Route, which included a stint on the Nürburgring. One car suffered reliability problems in the eleventh hour, but the other finished fourth overall.

Thus began Mazda's assault on European sports car racing. The Hiroshima company ran its first entry at Le Mans in 1970 (a Chevron with rotary power), and then entered its own cars beginning in 1974. More than a decade later, the company had proven to be one of the most

"Rotary engines are unreliable and not really competitive." Well, tell that to the 1991 Mazda/Renown Le Mans team. Their 787B with its four rotor power plant was and still is the only Far Eastern machine to win the event. *Autosport/LAT*

The RB26 engine that powered the 787B to overall victory is normally aspirated and features four rotors, with three sequential spark plugs for each of them. It makes 700 bhp from just 2.6 liters. *Autosport/LAT*

consistent finishers in the 24-hour race, garnering a 67 percent finish rate.

Even then, few people could have predicted the outcome of the 59th Le Mans 24 hours in 1991. Running a Nigel Stroud–designed chassis powered by a four-rotor, 2.6-liter, 700 bhp R26B engine, Mazda selected a lead driving team of F1 Racers Johnny Herbert and

MAZDA 787B
SPECIFICATIONS

Weight	1,830 lbs/830 kg	0–60 mph	n/a
Layout	ME R NA RWD	0–100 mph	n/a
Displacement	2.6 liters	Top speed	n/a
Max power	700 bhp @ 9000 rpm	Years in production	n/a
Max torque	459 lb/ft @ 6500 rpm	Cost in Gran Turismo	
Transmission	5-speed manual	credits	500,000

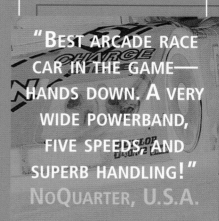

"BEST ARCADE RACE CAR IN THE GAME— HANDS DOWN. A VERY WIDE POWERBAND, FIVE SPEEDS, AND SUPERB HANDLING!"
NOQUARTER, U.S.A.

At this writing no other Japanese automaker has come close to matching Mazda's record at Le Mans, though Toyota did field its GT-One, which finished second in 1998. *Autosport/LAT*

Bertrand Gachot, along with Volker Weidler (the company also fielded two other 787Bs for the race). Many fans and experts predicted that all three cars would finish, which they did. Even so, few could have foreseen the events of lap 320 out of 362, when the distinctive green and orange number 55 Renown-sponsored 787B managed to muscle past the Porsches and Jaguars to take the lead. The car crossed the line 27 km ahead of the nearest TWR-prepped Jaguar and made history in the process.

Jaws dropped, critics were stunned, and the atmosphere both at the track and Mazda's headquarters that day was like none before. The company had done what 20 years earlier had been conceived as nigh impossible. Not only had Mazda beaten the Europeans at their own game, but it had done something that none of its Japanese rivals have yet managed —it had won the most prestigious motor race in the world!

When the Gachot/Herbet/Weidler machine qualified 17th for the starting grid in 1991, few could have predicted that 24 hours after the race began, it would cross the line to become the overall winner. *Autosport/LAT*

PAGANI ZONDA

It has a mid-mounted V-12 engine, provides exhilarating performance, costs more than a small country to buy, and is handcrafted in the charming town of Modena, Italy. If you're thinking Ferrari or Lamborghini, think again.

What we're referring to is the Pagani Zonda C12, one of the best machines of this ilk to emerge in recent years. Originating from an idea conceived back in 1988 by company founder Horacio Pagani and the late Juan Manuel Fangio, the Zonda took shape in remarkably little time. Key ingredients throughout its development included a Mercedes-Benz V-12 engine (mid-mounted of course), Formula 1 technology, and a quest to keep the car as light as possible.

What ultimately emerged in 2000 was a very beautiful and striking design with pronounced front fenders, forward mounted "fighter jet" style cockpit, wide track, and a long 2,730-mm wheelbase. The Zonda makes extensive use of carbon fiber (Pagani also runs a design composites business) and chrome moly steel tubing in its chassis construction. It also features such traditional supercar elements as a lightweight aluminum double-wishbone suspension and massive 355 mm-diameter Brembo disc brakes with four-piston calipers. Power comes courtesy of the aforementioned 6.0-liter V-12, mated to Pagani's own six-speed gearbox.

Cutting his teeth in the supercar world at Lamborghini, Horacio Pagani later set up his own operation, Pagani Automobili, just down the road. The Zonda C12 was the first vehicle to emerge. *AutoExpress/Evo*

Weighing in at just 1,250 kg and packing 389 bhp, the Zonda C12 astounded the critics and motoring press, not only with its amazing acceleration, but also with its agility and cornering manners. It was discernibly quicker through the twisties than many rivals, thus setting a new standard for handling in supercar circles.

Even though the company had shown it could take on the might of Ferrari and Lamborghini, Pagani didn't stop there. For 2001 it upped the ante and released the C12S. This new development featured more aggressive styling, but it was under the skin where the biggest changes were found. Behind the carbon fiber cockpit bulkhead was a bigger 7.0

AMG-prepped Mercedes V-12, which cranked out an incredible 542 bhp and 553 lb/ft of torque. Combined with a stronger six-speed gearbox and a curb weight nearly identical to

Horacio Pagani, friend of the late Juan Manuel Fangio, created the Zonda partly as a tribute to one of the greatest racing drivers ever. *AutoExpress/Evo*

C12S

PAGANI ZONDA C12S
SPECIFICATIONS

Weight	2,765 lbs/1,250 kg	0–60 mph	3.7 sec
Layout	ME V-12 NA RWD	0–100 mph	n/a
Displacement	7.0 liters	Top speed	220 mph
Max power	542 bhp @ 5550 rpm	Years in production	2001–
Max torque	553 lb/ft @ 4100 rpm	Cost in Gran Turismo	
Transmission	6-speed manual	credits	352,440

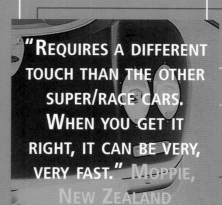

"REQUIRES A DIFFERENT TOUCH THAN THE OTHER SUPER/RACE CARS. WHEN YOU GET IT RIGHT, IT CAN BE VERY, VERY FAST." MOPPIE, NEW ZEALAND

The C12S features a hand-built 7.0-liter AMG monster that cranks out 542 bhp and propels the car from 0 to 60 mph in under 4 seconds and to a top speed of 220 mph. Despite its acceleration abilities, the Zonda is also incredibly tractable in everyday driving. *AutoExpress/Evo*

the standard C12, performance of the S in relation to the regular Zonda model was like comparing a Saturn V rocket to the SR-71 Blackbird.

British magazine *Evo* tested a C12S and managed to wring out a 0 to 60 mph time of 3.7 seconds (not far shy of the all-conquering, ultra-expensive McLaren F1) and a top speed of 220 mph. So impressed were the editors that they labeled the C12S their car of the year. From a periodical used to testing some of the fastest, most exotic machinery in the world, this was high praise indeed.

From every angle, the Zonda C12 has been blessed with aeronautical touches. From the fighter cockpit-style green house to the dramatic afterburner-like tailpipes at rear end, the car emphasizes beauty, power, and speed. *AutoExpress/Evo*

PANOZ ESPERANTE

Started by Danny Panoz in 1989, this Georgia-based company began building small, Lotus Super Seven-style roadsters powered by Ford V-8s. Soon, Danny's father, Don Panoz, decided he wanted a slice of the action. Son Danny had recently begun working on a true GT car, the Esperante, and Don decided to promote this new GT by building sports racers to compete in the FIA GT championship and the American Sports Car series.

He set up Panoz Motorsports right next to the Road Atlanta race circuit. Four GTR-1 cars were built by Reynard Special Vehicles Projects using big 6.0 Ford V-8 engines (a development of the old 351). Not only did Panoz decide to run with old-fashioned pushrod engines, but the GTR-1s were front-engined (whereas nearly all GT1 racers at the time had their motors placed behind the cockpit).

Panoz fielded one of these cars in the Professional Sports Car Championship Series, while the other three were run in the FIA GT championship by the British DPR and French DAMS teams. The PSCC car won at Road Atlanta on only its second outing, and a GTR-1 made the starting grid for the sixty-fifth running of the Le Mans 24 hours in 1997. After a strong performance (it was running consistently in the top 10) the distinctive-sounding GTR-1 suffered mechanical problems and retired with just 7 hours

Sounding for all the world like a big block top fuel dragster, the V-8 engined Panoz GTR-1 caused more than a few heads to turn when it debuted at Le Mans in 1997. *Autosport/LAT*

left to go. This first outing proved, however, that front-engined cars still had a place in GT endurance racing.

The following year, the big-motored monsters were back at Le Mans stronger than ever. David Brabham piloted the Number 12 Visteon GTR-1 to seventh overall, and a second car crossed the line in 13th place.

From there, things only got better. For 1999, Panoz unveiled open cockpit LMP-1 Roadsters, which cleaned up in the newly formed American Le Mans Series, winning at Portland, Oregon; Mosport, Ontario; and at Sebring. In 2000, an improved version, the LMP-1 S, was revealed and ran in the American Le Mans series and

In total, four GTR-1 chassis were originally built and three went to sports car teams in Europe. The fourth competed in the Professional Sports Car Championship in the United States, with considerable success. *Autosport/LAT*

GTR-1

PANOZ ESPERANTE GTR-1
SPECIFICATIONS

Weight	2,535 lbs/1,150 kg (est.)	0–60 mph	2.3 sec (est.)
Layout	FE V-8 NA RWD	0–100 mph	4.5 sec (est.)
Displacement	6.0 liters	Top speed	n/a
Max power	620 bhp @ 7000 rpm	Years in production	1996–98
Max torque	530 lb/ft @ 5500 rpm	Cost in Gran Turismo credits	2,000,000
Transmission	6-speed manual		

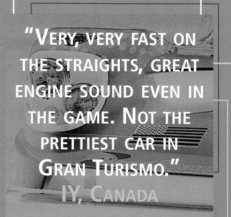

"VERY, VERY FAST ON THE STRAIGHTS, GREAT ENGINE SOUND EVEN IN THE GAME. NOT THE PRETTIEST CAR IN GRAN TURISMO."
IY, CANADA

After not finishing the first year, the Panoz team decided to try again at Le Mans at 1998, and this time things were much better. They finished 7th and 13th in the GT1 category, proving that these front-engine monsters had what it took .
Autosport/LAT

People often ask what the performance of a GT1 car is like "in real-world terms." To give you an idea, the Panoz GTR-1 and its LMP-07 successor, depending on gearing and setup, will accelerate to 60 mph from rest in around 2.3 seconds.
Autosport/LAT

also at Le Mans too, but sadly failed to finish. However, a Panoz did take the checkered flag at Germany's infamous Nürburgring later in the year.

The following season Panoz decided to experiment with the LMP 07, powered by the company's own 4.0-liter engine. However, complexity and teething troubles rendered the car uncompetitive in FIA GT events. After Le Mans, the company decided to bring back the LMP–1 S, with much success. In an arena that has seen car companies come and go like the wind, Panoz has proved it has

staying power and the right stuff to win big in competition, both at home and abroad.

SPOON SPORTS

One of the most talked-about sports cars of the new millennium is Honda's S2000. Built as a fiftieth anniversary machine to celebrate the founding of Soichiro Honda's company in 1949, it gave the average enthusiast the opportunity to own a bona fide touring-style sports car for the street.

Since then, both in Japan and around the world, Honda's little sports roadster has gained a very loyal following and has begun to demonstrate its potential for tuning. One firm at the forefront of this trend has been Spoon Sports, a Japanese company that has carved out a very respectable reputation for transforming decidedly ordinary Hondas into full-on competition machines.

The Spoon Sports S2000 is one of the company's more memorable creations. Built to compete in category 4 of Japan's N1 Super Taikyu Endurance series, the Spoon race cars were among the most consistent runners in their class for 2001. The company ultimately built six of the eight S2000s that competed in the series.

Like many racing events in Japan, N1 category 4 rules permit only a limited number of modifications. Although the Spoon S2000 features a hardtop, gutted interior, roll cage, and extra chassis bracing along with race-style coil-over suspension and patented cross-drilled brakes, plus ultra sticky Yokohama Advan

Honda's S2000 is a high-revving little sportster with superb chassis and brilliant handling. Spoon Sports recognized the car's potential and turned it into one of a very quick track machine. *John Russell*

Running in category 4 of the Japanese N1 Super Touring series, the Spoon S2000s have proved dominant—their rear-drive nature and almost perfect weight distribution makes them among the quickest and best-handling cars in their class. *John Russell*

S2000

SPOON SPORTS S2000
SPECIFICATIONS

Weight	2,315 lbs/1,050 kg	0–60 mph	6.1 sec (est.)
Layout	FE I-4 NA RWD	0–100 mph	14.2 sec (est.)
Displacement	2.0 liters	Top speed	n/a
Max power	271 bhp @ 9000 rpm	Years in production	2001–
Max torque	175 lb/ft @ 9000 rpm (est.)	Cost in Gran Turismo credits	50,000
Transmission	5-speed manual		

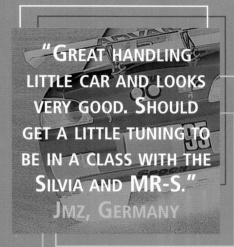

"GREAT HANDLING LITTLE CAR AND LOOKS VERY GOOD. SHOULD GET A LITTLE TUNING TO BE IN A CLASS WITH THE SILVIA AND MR-S."
JMZ, GERMANY

Endurance racing on any scale requires durability to win and thus engine mods in N1 are very restrictive. Thinner head gaskets, replacement ECUs, air filters, and valve springs are about the only items permitted.
John Russell

completed the Streets of Willow road course in 59.7 seconds—an amazing 2.3 seconds quicker than a supercharged street version and 5.4 seconds faster than a regular S2000.

Compared to a stock S2000, the Spoon Race car weighs nearly 400 lbs (181 kg) less and will accelerate to 60 mph almost a second quicker.
John Russell

slick tires, the 2.0-liter DOHC four is virtually stock, save for lightweight valve springs, an aftermarket head gasket, and Spoon's own ECU and air filter.

As durability is the name of the game in N1, Spoon also installs its own heavy-duty clutch and differential. Like its virtual counterpart in the game, the distinctive blue and yellow Polyphony Digital–sponsored

Spoon S2000 isn't among the quickest cars in a straight line, but thanks to its amazing lightweight chassis and sublime grip, it out-handles almost anything this side of a Le Mans racer. Combined with the car's excellent braking ability, this translates into astonishingly fast lap times. In fact, during a test by *Sport Compact Car* magazine, the Spoon S2000

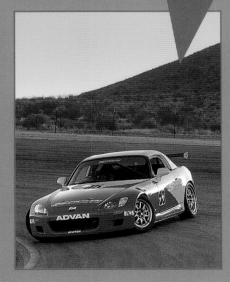

Escorts have been associated with rallying ever since the first European version of this car made its debut in 1968. Escorts took the WRC (World Rally Championship) crown in 1968, 1969, and from 1971–79. Finnish driver Ari Vantenen also took the 1980 WRC title driving a privately funded Escort RS 1800, even as Ford themselves began to concentrate on the Group B RS200.

Nearly a decade after Vantenen's triumph, Ford tried again. By now, Group A was top dog in the WRC, and in order for Ford to compete, it had to build a sizeable number of street replicas of its rally car. Because the Escort was at this time front-wheel drive, Ford utilized the old Sierra 4 x 4 chassis and mated it to the Escort three-door hatchback body.

Street versions featured a turbocharged 16-valve Cosworth-prepped 2.0-liter four-cylinder engine, five-speed manual transmission and a 4WD system operated by front and rear differentials and a central viscous coupling. Inside, the car was pure Escort, but on the outside the grocery-getter hatchback body was beefed up with bulging fenders (to clear the monster tires), a big front air dam, and a massive decklid spoiler.

The Cosworth became an instant favorite due to its incredible performance—with 227 bhp, acceleration from 0 to 60 mph took less than

The Escort Cossie was the logical successor to the formidable Ford Sierra in WRC and proved tremendously successful with drivers like Francois Delecour, Bruno Thiry, Carlos Sainz, and Juha Kankkunen at the wheel. *Autosport/LAT*

6 seconds and top speeds exceeded 140 mph. With 4WD and a well-balanced chassis, the car was also one of the best handling and quickest point-to-point automobiles you could buy in the early 1990s. Even today, few performance cars on the market can match it.

Unfortunately, the Cossie became a favored target for boy racers and thieves and soon became one of the most stolen cars in Europe. Insurance rates rocketed, sales plummeted, and the street version was discontinued in 1997.

In its debut WRC season in 1993, the car scored five victories, and the following year Frenchman Francois Delecour piloted a Works Escort to victory in the prestigious Monte Carlo Rally. Future rally legend Tommi

Built off the mainly rear-drive European Ford Sierra (Merkur XR4Ti in the United States) floorplan, the Cosworth had its twin cam four cylinder mounted longitudinally, causing many people to do a double-take when the hood was popped. *AutoExpress/Evo*

RS COSWORTH

FORD ESCORT RS COSWORTH
SPECIFICATIONS*

Weight	2,875 lbs/1,304 kg	0–60 mph	5.8 sec
Layout	FE I-4T AWD	0–100 mph	n/a
Displacement	2.0 liters	Top speed	143 mph
Max power	227 bhp @ 6250 rpm	Years in production	1991–97
Max torque	224 lb/ft @ 3500 rpm	Cost in Gran Turismo credits	87,500
Transmission	5-speed manual		

* refers to Street version

> "I USED THE COSSIE TO FINISH THE RALLY SECTION. FULLY POWERED AND TUNED, I THINK IT IS THE ONE TO BEAT IN THIS SECTION."
> NoQuarter, U.S.A.

The massive rear wing was a major part in the car's boy racer appeal but could be deleted in some markets at the buyer's request. *AutoExpress/Evo*

In 1999, the new Focus WRC replaced the Escort. Even today, the Cossie remains a recognized motoring symbol across the globe. You may love it, you may hate it, but you can't deny that it made a significant impact on the automotive landscape.

By 1997, the Escort was becoming outclassed in World Championship Rallying, but works drivers Carlos Sainz and Juha Kankkunen still managed to put in some respectable performances. *Autosport/LAT*

Makinen also scored his first-ever WRC victory in 1994 at the 1000 Lakes with a Cosworth.

By 1997, the Cosworth had morphed into the Escort WRC and with experienced drivers Carlos Sainz and Juha Kankkunen, the Works/Repsol team finished 1-2 in the Acropolis Rally and the Rally of Indonesia, with Sainz finishing third in the Championship.

LANCIA DELTA

This Italian 4WD monster emerged from surprisingly humble origins. The Delta was a sensible Italian family hatchback with boxy lines and fairly decent handling. Its only claim to fame in the early years was winning the European Car of the Year award for 1979.

Seven years later, the humble Lancia underwent a transformation. Engineers combined a 2.0 turbocharged engine with a Ferguson four-wheel drive system (including a torque-splitting center differential), resulting in the 165 bhp HF 4WD Turbo. Lancia now had the perfect platform with which to enter Group A World Championship Rallying.

Several months later, a competition version—dubbed Integrale—was in action. Right from the start the boxy little Lancia was a champ. The distinctive Martini-sponsored white, blue, and red cars finished a smashing 1-2 in Monte Carlo, with drivers Miki Baision and Juha Kankkunen at the wheel. Further wins in Portugal, Greece, Argentina, Finland (1000 Lakes), San Remo, and Britain (RAC) saw Lancia walk away with the constructor's title and Kankkunen gaining his second WRC crown.

Following this tremendous success, a street HF Integrale was released in November 1987. It was similar to the old HF 4WD but featured more aggressive styling, with bulging fenders and an engine tuned to produce 185 bhp, resulting in rocket-like

In the late 1980s, World Championship Rally pretty much meant one thing—Integrale. Lancia's factory-backed Martini Deltas ruled the roost, winning nearly everything in sight. *Autosport/LAT*

acceleration times (0 to 60 mph in 6.6 seconds anyone?)

Back on the rally front, Lancia again won the constructor's title and Baision the driver's cup for 1988. In 1989, the Works Martini Team once again obliterated the competition. For the next three years, it was a similar picture, with both the Works team and its drivers coming out on top.

Toward the end of 1989, the company launched an improved

16-valve Integrale for street use, which featured bigger wheels and tires, a revised 4WD system with a more rearward torque bias, and a tuned 2.0-liter four now cranking out 200 bhp, plus a hydraulic clutch and standard ABS brakes. In late 1991 (with Lancia and Kankkunen on their way to another WRC title), the Evolution brought a wider track, revised bodywork, tweaked rear suspension, and stouter steering.

Ultimate street Integrale was the Evo II that arrived in 1993. Underhood, the 2.0-liter intercooled four cranked out an impressive 215 bhp—good for 0 to 60 in 5.8 seconds. *AutoExpress/Evo*

HF INTEGRALE

LANCIA DELTA HF INTEGRALE
SPECIFICATIONS*

Weight	2,976 lbs/1,350 kg	0–60 mph	5.7 sec
Layout	FE I-4T AWD	0–100 mph	n/a
Displacement	2.0 liters	Top speed	137 mph (est.)
Max power	215 bhp @ 5750 rpm	Years in production	1987–1995
Max torque	220 lb/ft @ 3500 rpm	Cost in Gran Turismo	
Transmission	5-speed manual	credits	500,000

* refers to Evolution II street model

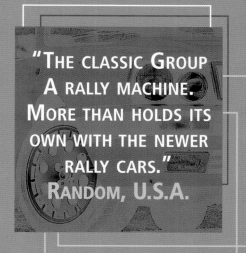

"THE CLASSIC GROUP A RALLY MACHINE. MORE THAN HOLDS ITS OWN WITH THE NEWER RALLY CARS." RANDOM, U.S.A.

As per Group A rules, the Rally Integrale had to have a street counterpart. In late 1989 the road version got bigger wheels and tires, plus a new 16-valve engine—good enough to propel the little hatchback from 0 to 60 mph in 6 seconds flat. *National Motor Museum, Beaulieu*

following May boasting 215 bhp. The automotive press was quick to heap praise on the EVO II, and one of the more respected magazines even labeled it as "one of the finest cars ever built." Anyone who has ever had the pleasure of driving an Integrale would say exactly the same.

As it was on the street, the 16-valve Integrale was just as dominant on the Rally Circuit in 1990. Miki Baision was instrumental in the Lancia team, gaining its fourth straight Constructor's championship title that year. *Autosport/LAT*

In honor of its incredible success in rallying, Lancia released two limited-edition Integrales in 1991 and 1992, which featured special upholstery, white wheels, and paint with Martini-style striping.

Lancia officially withdrew from the rally circuit in 1992, but this didn't stop the ultimate Integrale. The Evolution II appeared in showrooms the

Like many rally cars, the Impreza started out as little more than a small sedan/wagon when launched in late 1992. Subaru figured it would be the perfect foundation with which to plan an all-out assault on the WRC. As per the rules, Subaru built a road-going counterpart. The first result was the 240 bhp WRX turbo, which went on sale in Japan in November 1992. For the 1994 WRC season, Subaru managed to sign 1992 world champion Carlos Sainz, pairing him up with quick Scotsman Colin McRae.

At the same time, the WRX STi was released in Japan. Outwardly similar to its predecessor, the STi featured a reworked engine with lighter pistons and a tweaked intercooler and ECU. Power output was 250 bhp, but many sources reported the car made far more. In the 1994 rally season, Sainz won the Acropolis Rally and McRae won the New Zealand and British RAC events.

When the season ended, Subaru launched a further road-going development of the WRX—the RA STi, featuring 275 bhp, quicker steering, and a revised 4WD system with more rearward torque bias. In 1995, the blue and yellow cars of the Prodrive Works team became a serious force. Sainz won the season opener at Monte Carlo, and consistent results all year gave Subaru the constructor's championship and McRae the drivers' title.

A great rival to the all-conquering Lancer Evolution series is Subaru's Impreza WRX STi, seen here in 2002 form. *AutoExpress/Evo*

Under the hood is a distinct Subaru trademark: a water-cooled flat four engine. With its horizontally opposed cylinders, it emits a sound like no other. *AutoExpress/Evo*

To commemorate its WRC victory, Subaru created the STi V-limited, with special paint (including gold wheels), embroidery, and badging. Just 1,000 were built. A two-door STi–R was released in early 1997 along with a further V-limited sedan/wagon as a salute to the company's second-straight manufacturer's title of 1996.

In 1998, Subaru launched the two-door WRX STi 22B. Rated at 276 bhp and only available in Sonic Blue, this car was a monster—posting 0 to 60 mph in 5 seconds. This was followed by the 22B-based limited edition

WRC/WRX STi

SUBARU IMREZA WRC/WRX STi
SPECIFICATIONS

Weight	3,153 lbs/1,430 kg	0–60 mph	4.8 sec
Layout	FE H-4T AWD	0–100 mph	13.0 sec
Displacement	2.0 liters	Top speed	140 mph
Max power	276 bhp @ 6400 rpm	Years in production	2000-
Max torque	275 lb/ft @ 4000 rpm	Cost in Gran Turismo	
Transmission	6-speed manual	credits	31,980

* refers to Street version

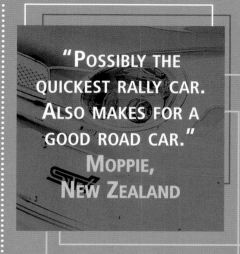

"POSSIBLY THE QUICKEST RALLY CAR. ALSO MAKES FOR A GOOD ROAD CAR."
MOPPIE, NEW ZEALAND

Introduced to World Championship Rallying in 1994, it wasn't long before the Prodrive built Imprezas became a dominant force. Colin McRae and later Richard Burns (seen here) became household names in Europe and around the globe. *John Russell*

In the WRC, after losing to Peugeot and Marcus Gronholm in 2000, Prodrive and Richard Burns took the world championship title and yet another constructor's cup. On the street, the surefooted and immensely fun-to-drive Impreza STi (now capable of 0 to 60 mph in 4.8 seconds) proved more popular than ever.

RB-5 in 1999, named for lead driver Richard Burns. The next and final first-generation Impreza variant was the crazy P1, built by Prodrive. It was the quickest and best-handling Impreza so far, capable of reaching 100 mph from a standstill in 14.6 seconds. This was about the closet thing you could get to piloting a full-blown WRC car.

For 2001, Subaru launched a revamped Impreza (including WRX and STi), plus it finally saw fit to send the WRX version to the United States and Canada.

For the 2001 season Burns and Prodrive clinched the championship after steady accumulation of points and in 2002, Norwegian driver Petter Solberg, after several attempts, finally achieved victory in the RAC. *John Russell*

At one time, the biggest Japanese name in World Championship rallying was Toyota, whose Team Europe fielded the remarkable Celica GT-Four. It all started in October 1986 with the Japanese launch of a 4WD Celica, with its 2.0-liter turbocharged and intercooled 185 bhp four-cylinder engine (the most powerful in Japan up to that time), and a full-time all-wheel drive system. Costing almost three million yen, it was expensive, but Toyota really had one goal with the GT-Four: win the World Rally Championship.

The Group A Celica debuted at the 1988 Tour De Course. With the Lancias still walking all over the competition, it would take awhile for Toyota to be seriously competitive, but a third-place finish in the Lombard RAC was encouraging. By this stage, the road-going GT-Four had also hit European and American shores.

In the WRC, Toyota made some serious progress the following year—Juha Kankkunen won in Australia in a non-works car, demonstrating the Celica's potential. By 1990, newly signed lead works driver, Spaniard Carlos Sainz, performed well enough during the season to clinch the driver's championship.

In the meantime, Toyota launched a new fifth-generation Celica, similar under the skin to its predecessor but with dramatic new styling. The top dog turbocharged GT-Four

Distinguished from lesser versions of Toyota's sporty coupe by its central hood scoop and massive rear wing, the sixth-generation GT-Four was a fast, exclusive machine seldom seen on Western roads. *Autosport/LAT*

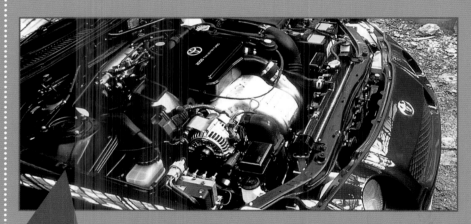

With 239 bhp on tap from its turbocharged and intercooled 2.0-liter four, the 1994–97 Celica GT-Four was the quickest and most refined of these AWD turbocharged Toyota coupes. Sadly it was also the last. *Autosport/LAT*

returned, now packing an impressive 225 bhp, thanks to turbo tweaks and the addition of an air-to-air intercooler.

At the 1992 Monte Carlo, Toyota unveiled the fifth-generation-based WRC, and Sainz drove it to his second world title. As a result, Toyota introduced a special edition Carlos Sainz Celica and later the GT-Four RC (signifying Rally Competition). This special Celica featured a redesigned exhaust, new intercooler, and other goodies resulting in 235 bhp. As per regulations, 500 were built.

In 1993, Toyota took the WRC constructors' cup, with Juha Kankkunen winning the driver's championship. The following

GT-FOUR

TOYOTA CELICA GT-FOUR
SPECIFICATIONS

Weight	3,298 lbs/1,496 kg	0–60 mph	5.2 sec
Layout	FE I-4T AWD	0–100 mph	n/a
Displacement	2.0 liters	Top speed	143 mph
Max power	239 bhp @ 6000 rpm	Years in production	1994–97
Max torque	223 lb/ft @ 4000 rpm	Cost in Gran Turismo	
Transmission	5-speed manual	credits	32,660/75,000

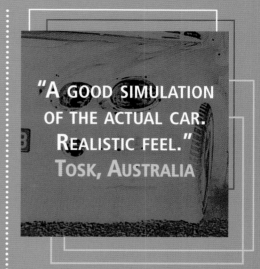

"A GOOD SIMULATION OF THE ACTUAL CAR. REALISTIC FEEL."
TOSK, AUSTRALIA

Toyota's success could be contributed to the driving talent of Juha Kankkunen and Didier Auriol (seen here in the 1995 Swedish Rally) as well as the Celica's excellent reliability. *Autosport/LAT*

When the Toyota works team used the European Corolla for its 1998 WRC effort, the Celica GT-Four was finally put out to pasture. Rare when new and even more so today, it remains an example of that rare breed—a blindingly quick rally special with comfort and refinement to match. It's a shame so few were built.

year saw a repeat, with Didier Auriol taking the championship.

Toyota rally fever continued with the sixth-generation turbocharged and intercooled GT-Four, which had fixed circular headlights, a big hood scoop and a massive rear wing, and was the fastest and smoothest Celica yet. Capable of performing the 0 to 60 mph run in 5.9 seconds and with a top end close to 155 mph, the car's supple ride and ample creature comforts, along with standard ABS, made this 4WD homologation especially easy to live with on a regular basis.

In the WRC the distinctive Castrol-sponsored works Celicas cars were dominant in the early 1990s, winning two constructor's championships and propelling Carlos Sainz and Juha Kankkunen to driver's titles between then and 1995. *Autosport/LAT*

ASTON MARTIN

This 2002 grand tourer from bespoke automaker Aston Martin was designed to *vanquish* the competition. Originating from the Vantage concept of 1998, this 6.0-liter V-12-engined monster capitalized on Aston's rich heritage and racing past, wrapped up in a take-no-prisoners package for the new millennium. The Vanquish is like a muscle-bound athlete dressed in a tailored London Saville Row suit.

Styled by Ian McCallum, the brawny shape clearly maintains a link to past Astons (especially at the front), but it was clearly designed with the present and future in mind. Inside, it boasts all the refinement and class expected of an Aston Martin, with quality materials, plenty of British Connolly leather, and even a parking brake located by the sill on the driver's side in classic European style.

However, it's the technology employed under the skin that really gives this car its defining character. The V-12 engine, an all-aluminum piece with four overhead cams, 32 valves and electronic sequential fuel injection, cranks out a whopping 460 bhp and 400 lb/ft of torque. Behind it is a six-speed gearbox with Magneti-Marelli electronic sequential shift, operated via paddles attached to the steering wheel (like the Ferrari 360 and 550/575 F1), and a true racing-style double wishbone suspension with the upper and lower arms cast from aluminum

Aston Martin's new Vanquish supercar made a huge splash with the public due to its role as James Bond's wheels in the movie *Die Another Day*. With a production run of just 200 per year worldwide, however, it remained a rare and exclusive automobile in the company's long-standing tradition. *AutoExpress/Evo*

One of the key ingredients to this Aston's thundering performance is its monster 6.0-liter V12. It makes an impressive 460 bhp at a very usable 6500 rpm and provides silky smooth and progressive power delivery. *AutoExpress/Evo*

to save weight. Brakes are massive Brembos (14 inches in front, 13 in the rear). The 19-inch wheels, 255/40/19 front and 285/40/19 rear tires, are equally monstrous.

With a curb weight of more than 4,110 lbs (1864 kg), the Vanquish isn't exactly light. What is most astonishing is that the Vanquish is amazingly entertaining to drive on narrow coastal and country roads, with far greater poise and agility than its size and weight should permit. The V-12 is velvety smooth, and the sequential shift is surprisingly easy to use.

VANQUISH

ASTON MARTIN VANQUISH
SPECIFICATIONS

Weight	4,110 lbs/1,864 kg	0–60 mph	4.7 sec
Layout	FE V-12 NA RWD	0–100 mph	10.8 sec
Displacement	6.0 liters	Top speed	190 mph
Max power	460 bhp @ 6500 rpm	Years in production	2001–
Max torque	400 lb/ft @ 5000 rpm	Cost in Gran Turismo credits	Prize Car
Transmission	6-speed manual		

> "WOW! GREAT HANDLING AND POWER! HAVEN'T TRIED TUNING ONE—DOESN'T NEED IT."
> RANDOM, U.S.A.

Inside, the Vanquish features all the comfort and convenience expected. The seats and much of the interior are stitched from the finest British Connolly leather and with traditional Willow carpeting on the floor. Extensive use of brushed aluminum, however, roots this car firmly in the early twenty-first century. *AutoExpress/Evo*

chosen as James Bond's ride in *Die Another Day*, returning Aston Martin to its rightful role as the personal transportation of Britain's top spy hero.

Despite its size and weight, the Vanquish is superb at corner carving. Massive 19-inch wheels and tires not only look good but—combined with a well-engineered suspension and chassis—give the car unworldly levels of grip and handling. *AutoExpress/Evo*

Pressing your right foot onto the drive-by-wire operated accelerator brings 60 mph in a rapid 4.7 seconds. One hundred mph comes up in a shade over 10. As the speed increases, the big Aston remains as stable as a rock and will haul all the way up to 190 mph. Ride and comfort are exemplary at all times.

The Vanquish is such a star performer that, in a 2002 comparison test, it out-accelerated, out-handled, and out-braked perhaps its greatest rival—the hallowed Ferrari 575. The biggest compliment of all was that the Vanquish was

AUDI S4

The folks from Ingolstadt have a fairly long history of producing interesting (and quick) production cars using the company's patented Quattro all-wheel drive system. One of the best loved is the S4, derived from Audi's best-selling A4 compact sedan.

In the mid 1990s, Audi began a new assault on the racing world via its motorsports division, particularly in sports and touring car events. "Race on Sunday, sell on Monday" is an age-old slogan in the automotive world, and Audi, like many others, decided to make the connection between its road cars and the company's racing efforts—hence the S line of automobiles.

The S4, bowing in 1996, was essentially an A4 Quattro on steroids. Under the hood it had a 2.7-liter twin-turbo V-6 borrowed from the new A6 and tuned to deliver 270 bhp (250 in U.S. trim). Other goodies included stiffened suspension, bigger brakes, and massive 17-inch race-style rims on ultra-low profile tires. Outwardly, the S4 differed from its lesser stablemates with a unique front air dam and rocker panel extensions.

Despite these alterations, the S4 was still quite the sleeper—understated from the outside but with the heart of a lion beneath. Hitting the loud pedal erased any doubts that this was a serious performer. With spades of torque from

Audi's original S4, launched in 1996, paid homage to its legendary RS2 predecessor. Although the S4 was a milder machine, it still could match several bespoke super cars in acceleration testing, yet return more than 20 mpg. *Jerry Heasley*

the blown V-6, the car could hit 60 mph in about 5.5 seconds and the quarter mile in just over 14. It also proved to be a civilized high-speed carriage capable of wafting its occupants along in total comfort at triple-digit speeds. With its compliant chassis, torsion beam suspension and quick steering, and Quattro system with its Torsen (torque

The S4's twin turbo V-6 (a variation of which was also used in the bigger A6 sedan), was rated at 270 bhp in Europe and 250 bhp in North America, but performance differences between the two versions were marginal. *Jerry Heasley*

QUATTRO

AUDI S4 QUATTRO
SPECIFICATIONS*

Weight	3,333 lbs/1,512 kg	0–60 mph	5.5 sec
Layout	FE V-6TT AWD	0–100 mph	n/a
Displacement	2.7 liters	Top speed	155 mph
Max power	270 bhp @ 5800 rpm	Years in production	1996–2001
Max torque	295 lb/ft @ 3600 rpm	Cost in Gran Turismo credits	Prize Car
Transmission	6-speed manual		

* refers to European version

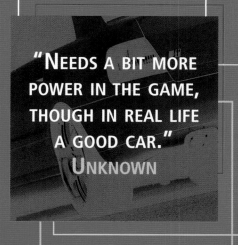

"NEEDS A BIT MORE POWER IN THE GAME, THOUGH IN REAL LIFE A GOOD CAR." UNKNOWN

Top speed on the S4 was electronically limited to 155 mph as per German requirements, but many testers believe the car was capable of far more. *Jerry Heasley*

Along with its lesser A4 stablemates, the original S4 was retired in 2001 but paved the way for a new version, launched in 2003, that boasted a 4.2-liter normally aspirated V8. *Jerry Heasley*

sensing) differentials, the S4 was also a star performer on switchback roads. In press testing, it proved tremendously quick around the road course, able to generate speeds and lap times equal to if not better than many so-called "sports" cars. Unlike many of these machines, however, the Audi is a performance car for all seasons and all conditions.

With its bright orange paint, forward-jutting air dam, prominent deck spoiler, and side-mounted exhaust—the 2000 Mustang Cobra R is about as subtle as a fire truck. When you fire up its mighty 5.4-liter DOHC V8, you're greeted with a thundering yet melodious sound.

Inside its unmistakably a Mustang, but it's all business—no radio, A/C, or rear seat. You can drive it on the street, but the Cobra R was essentially built for one thing in mind: to tear up in SCCA showroom stock racing. In order for the car to compete, Ford's SVT (Special Vehicle Team—its enthusiast division) had to build the car as a street-going race-ready machine for public sale. Not surprisingly, the terms "public" and "street" are used loosely—after all, you needed special racing credentials (like an SCCA license) to purchase a Cobra R. What you got for your $55,000 was unlike any other street-going factory-built Mustang. All you needed to take it racing was a set of sponsor stickers and a racing number!

Like its 1993 and 1995 predecessors, the 2000 Cobra R combined the best off-the-shelf factory parts to create a truly memorable performance machine. Ford's Special Vehicle Engineering—led by Mustang missionary John Coletti—started with the 1999 Mustang Cobra (including its independent rear suspension) as the basis for the mighty R, but from there things

Big, brawny, and brash, the 2000 Cobra R was in every sense the ultimate production version of the SN95 Mustang. It was also very exclusive, as only 300 were built. *Ford Motor Company (via Jerry Heasley)*

got seriously wild. More power meant more displacement, but instead of hopping up the 4.6-V-8 they decided to shoehorn in its bigger 5.4-liter brother—still with four overhead cams.

The five-speed transmission was replaced by a heavy-duty six-speed, and both the chassis and suspension were beefed up to cope with the extra power—some 385 horses. In the

All 2000 Mustang Cobra Rs came in any color you liked so long as it was orange. Massive 18-inch wheels, BF Goodrich G-Force rubber, and a dual-side exiting Borla exhaust were standard on this monster. *Ford Motor Company (via Jerry Heasley)*

COBRA R

FORD MUSTANG COBRA R
SPECIFICATIONS

Weight	3,590 lbs/1,628 kg	0–60 mph	4.8 sec
Layout	FE V-8 NA RWD	0–100 mph	n/a
Displacement	5.4 liters	Top speed	165 mph (est.)
Max power	385 bhp @ 6250 rpm	Years in production	2000
Max torque	385 lb/ft @ 4250 rpm	Cost in Gran Turismo credits	Prize Car
Transmission	6-speed manual		

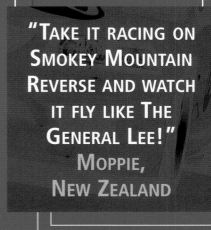

"TAKE IT RACING ON SMOKEY MOUNTAIN REVERSE AND WATCH IT FLY LIKE THE GENERAL LEE!"
MOPPIE,
NEW ZEALAND

Like its 1995 predecessor, the 2000 Cobra was significant in having the biggest factory-installed engine of all 1999–04 Mustangs under its intimidating, bulging hood. *Ford Motor Company (via Jerry Heasley)*

V-8 Mustangs gained a reputation as bang-for-the-buck street kings in the late 1980s. This reputation faded as the car gained weight and increased in price the following decade. The Cobra R (limited edition, street-legal race car or not) returned the Mustang to its rightful place at the top of the automotive food chain, and for that it deserves the ultimate in respect.

quarter mile, the Cobra R would run 12 seconds all day long with a set of slicks (despite a road racing suspension), though it was on the road course where it truly shined. In a comparison test, *Motor Trend* magazine recorded a 1.00 lateral g on the skidpad, which was greater than all the other cars in the test (including the Ferrari 360 Modena, Dodge Viper ACR, and Porsche 911 Turbo—all of which cost considerably more).

Like the engine, chassis and suspension mods were equally over-the-top. Each Cobra R had massive Brembo brakes, Eibach springs, and Bilstein shocks, among other things. *Ford Motor Company (via Jerry Heasley)*

HONDA NSX-R

During the late 1980s, Honda was sailing on the crest of a wave. The company's engines had made it a legend in Formula 1 circles, and around the world Honda had gained a savvy reputation for reliable, good-quality cars—things were indeed good.

What better way to demonstrate the company's technological tour de force than by building a bona fide mid-engined supercar? Called NSX (and sold under both Acura and Honda brands), it arrived on the scene in 1990 to much critical acclaim. It was low and lithe, with a mid-mounted 3.0-liter DOHC V-6 engine and one of the most civilized interiors yet seen in a supercar. Honda spent hours on development work and track testing at the Nürburgring circuit in Germany, and the result was one of the finest-handling automobiles the world had ever seen. In fact several magazines went on to label the NSX as the world's best handling car—a high accolade indeed, considering that at the time few people could really take the idea of a Japanese-designed and -built supercar seriously.

With each passing year, Honda continued to prove the critics wrong as the NSX improved and matured like a fine wine. In 1992, a special lightweight version—the Type-R—was released. It was essentially a homologation special for Japan's burgeoning Super Touring and Endurance racing series. It was

First shown at Tokyo in 2001, the latest NSX-R was built to qualify the car for the All Japan Grand Touring Championship (JGTC) and was stripped of all unnecessary equipment to make it as light as possible. *Honda*

essentially the same as a regular NSX, but all unnecessary features were removed in the quest to save weight and increase performance. The Type-R was a raw, hard-edged performance machine and the first in the Acura/Honda line to wear this coveted badge.

In 2001, the NSX received a thorough modernization, though outwardly, save for fixed headlights instead of pop-ups, it looked much the same. Like it

had done ten years prior, Honda decided to build another R version to compete in the Japanese Touring Car Championship against the factory-backed teams from Nissan and Toyota. The new NSX-R features a carbon fiber hood and rear spoiler, along with reduced sound deadening and lighter interior carpeting. The V-6 (now displacing 3.2 liters), while rated at the same 280 bhp as other NSXs, boasts

Although the R model's V-6 displaces the same 3.2 liters beneath its striking red cam covers and is rated at the same 280 bhp as the standard NSX motor, it is some ten percent lighter and noticeably more responsive through the rev range. *Honda*

HONDA NSX-R
SPECIFICATIONS

Weight	2,864 lbs/1,299 kg	0–60 mph		4.3 sec
Layout	ME V-6 NA RWD	0–100 mph		9.9 sec
Displacement	3.5 liters	Top speed		175 mph
Max power	350 bhp @ 6500 rpm	Years in production		1999–2000
Max torque	295 lb/ft @ 4250 rpm	Cost in Gran Turismo		
Transmission	6-speed manual	credits		113,540

> "LIKE IN REAL LIFE, ONE OF THE MOST UNDERRATED CARS IN GRAN TURISMO. HANDLING IS SIMPLY BRILLIANT!"
> UNKNOWN

One of the easiest ways to spot the revamped 2002 NSX is by its fixed projector beam headlights, which replaced the heavier pop-up units. *AutoExpress/Evo (regular NSX)*

line. Possibly the only drawback of this car is availability. The Japanese keep nearly every NSX-R to themselves.

lighter internals—helping it to rev more quickly.

Weighing in at some 120 kg less than a regular NSX, the R version is a blistering performer. Sixty mph can be reached in a claimed 4.4 seconds, and its top speed is 168 mph. A stiffer suspension and revised aerodynamics also mean it is the best-handling NSX yet— capable of utterly insane cornering speeds—yet it's still remarkably docile on twisting sections, rarely stepping out of

NSX-R-unique items include the 17-inch wheels, 215/40ZR/17 and 255/40ZR/17 tires (front and rear respectively), and carbon fiber front hood pieces and rear spoiler. You also had a choice of color—anything you wanted as long as it was white. *Honda*

History has a tendency to repeat itself, and the Clio Sport V6 is a prime example. In the early 1980s, Renault built the monstrous R5 turbo (spun off its little front-drive hatchback) to compete in World Championship Rallying, which it did with much success. The street counterpart to the Maxi, as it was called, was rare, expensive, fast, and unlike anything on the road at the time. Even today, the Renault 5 Turbo and its Turbo 2 successor are much admired.

When Renault decided to look for a successor to the distinctive Sport Spider in the one-make Renault Trophy race series, the company found inspiration in the past. Deciding to use the best-selling Clio II (itself originally a replacement for the Renault 5) as the basis for its new racer, France's No. 1 automaker, in conjunction with Tom Walkinshaw Racing, employed similar tactics to the old Renault 5 Turbo—turning a front-engined, front-drive hatchback into a mid-engined, rear-drive monster.

This required almost a total re-engineering of the Clio chassis and suspension in order to install a 230 bhp 3.0 liter V-6 with a six-speed transmission. Like the chassis, the body was also heavily revised. It is much wider and more muscular, with scoops aft the doors to direct air into the twin radiators. Apart from the hood and basic shell, all other body panels were manufactured

It's a sport compact, Jim, but not as we know it! Taking the concept of hot hatch/sport compact to a whole new level was the mighty Clio Sport V6. *AutoExpress/Evo*

from composites to keep weight as low as possible.

At the 1998 Paris Auto Salon, Renault displayed a prototype that generated much interest by the press and public. A production version followed some months later.

When you walk up to a Sport V6, it looks like something out of a Japanese street racing cartoon, with its massive wheels and bulging bodywork. With just two seats inside and a massive V-6 where the trunk used to be, it ain't exactly practical, either. All that ceases to matter out on the open road. It displays driving characteristics similar to the old R5 Turbo, though it's far more refined. Acceleration is amazing (0 to 60 mph in 5.8 seconds), and the mid-engined layout translates to brilliant handling both on the road and racetrack. However, with plenty of torque going to the back tires and the

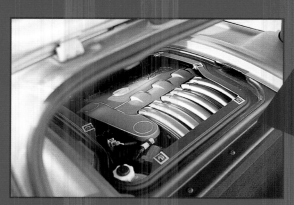

The formidable V-6 engine was derived from the one used in the top-level Laguna, Renault's mainstream family sedan. For the Clio V6, it was rated at 230 bhp and 221 lb/ft of torque. *AutoExpress/Evo*

SPORT V6

RENAULT CLIO SPORT V6
SPECIFICATIONS

Weight	2,943 lbs/1,335 kg	0–60 mph	5.8 sec
Layout	ME V-6 NA RWD	0–100 mph	17.0 sec
Displacement	3.0 liters	Top speed	145 mph
Max power	230 bhp @ 6000 rpm	Years in production	2000–
Max torque	221 lb/ft @ 3750 rpm	Cost in Gran Turismo credits	Prize Car
Transmission	6-speed manual		

> "JUST BEAUTIFUL, ONE OF THE BEST ROAD CARS IN THE GAME. A SOFT SEMI-RACE SUSPENSION AND 380 BHP WILL SEE IT COMPETE WITH JGTC CARS ON ANY CIRCUIT."
> MOPPIE, NEW ZEALAND

Although it resembled a boy racer's dream come true, the Clio Sport V6 was the essential baby supercar, far quicker and better handling than any traditional hot hatch. *AutoExpress/Evo*

With the mid-mounted V-6 and a wonderfully balanced chassis, the Clio Sport had more than enough performance to back up its racy looks—0 to 60 mph in just 5.8 seconds, and a top speed of 145 mph was just the icing on the cake. *AutoExpress/Evo*

whole car weighing just 1,335 kg, things can get a bit tricky (especially on slippery surfaces), as the tail has a tendency to let go fairly easily. You do need to keep your wits about you.

Sold new for around £25,000, the Clio Sport V6 is a baby supercar and a performance bargain in every sense of the word. There are virtually no other vehicles in this price category that offer the same kind of ownership and driving experience.

On your progression through Simulation mode in Gran Turismo 3 A-spec, perhaps the most interesting cars you can win are the ultra-secret F1 racers. One of the most powerful is the mysterious F686M. Think back to the 1986 Formula 1 Grand Prix season and you'll recognize it as none other than the turbocharged Williams Honda FW11.

Frank Williams made a deal with Honda to supply engines for his team during the 1983 season. The team's first turbo car, the FW09, appeared at the South African Grand Prix toward the end of the year, and Finn Keke Rosberg managed a fifth-place finish. The following year, the Honda motors were plagued by reliability problems, though for 1985 things improved considerably. With new sponsorship and a new car (the FW10—designed by Patrick Head and featuring the team's first carbon fiber chassis), plus the signing of Briton Nigel Mansell (previously with Lotus) to partner Rosberg, things definitely looked up. Although McLaren and Alain Prost continued to dominate, Williams got new Honda V-6 engines in time for Canada, and the new package proved competitive, helping the team to several wins in the latter part of the season.

For 1986, Williams signed former World Champion Nelson Piquet to partner Mansell. The

Between 1983 and 1987, FIA regulations in Formula 1 stipulated that cars be powered by 1.5-liter turbocharged engines. During the 1986 season, the Williams Honda FW11 proved the machine to beat. *Autosport/LAT*

team's sleek new FW11, powered by Honda's RA166 turbo V-6, proved to be a world-beater. In the opening round in Brazil, Piquet swept by Ayrton Senna to give the FW11 its first victory.

As the season progressed, the distinctive blue, yellow, and white cars proved to be the dominant force. By the final round of the season, Piquet and Mansell had won nine races between them. The season finale in Adelaide, Australia, proved to be one of the most exciting F1 races of the decade. Prost was first to the checkered flag, securing his second World Championship title by the slimmest of margins. Williams, however,

Depending on conditions, these 1.5-liter engines could make anywhere from 700 to 1,000 bhp for qualifying and racing but were hard on parts. Honda managed to eliminate many reliability problems on its RA166 twin turbo, enabling the Williams and later the McLaren team to totally dominate. *Autosport/LAT*

FW 11 (F686M)

WILLIAMS HONDA FW 11 (F686M)
SPECIFICATIONS

Weight	1,190 lbs/540 kg	0–60 mph	n/a
Layout	ME V-6TT RWD	0–100 mph	n/a
Displacement	1.5 liters	Power to weight ratio:	0.583
Max power	926 bhp @ 12,500 rpm	Top speed	n/a
Max torque	562 lb/ft @ 10,500 rpm	Years in production	1986
Transmission	6-speed manual	Cost in Gran Turismo credits	Prize Car

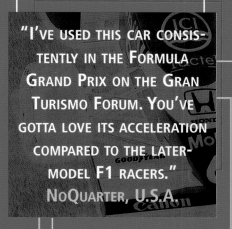

"I'VE USED THIS CAR CONSISTENTLY IN THE FORMULA GRAND PRIX ON THE GRAN TURISMO FORUM. YOU'VE GOTTA LOVE ITS ACCELERATION COMPARED TO THE LATER-MODEL F1 RACERS."
NoQUARTER, U.S.A.

Nigel Mansell (red number 5) on his way to victory in the British Grand Prix, Brands Hatch, 1986. Mansell's luck began to turn after signing with Williams, and the 1986 season left no doubt that he was a Grand Prix star. *Autosport/LAT*

had garnered enough points in the season to win the Constructor's Cup.

The following season, Williams fielded an improved version—the FW11B—and both the team and Piquet won their respective championships. Today, the Williams Honda FW11 remains a symbol of one of the most intriguing eras in Grand Prix racing.

Compared to a current F1 car, this turbocharged racer is a raw, untamed beast. It boasts a wide track, full slick tires, and its tiny 1.5-liter twin turbo engine makes 926 bhp

at 12,500 rpm. The cockpit provides little in the way of padding or side protection for the driver, and a good old-fashioned six-speed manual with a stubby shifter is located close to the driver's right hand. This car requires tremendous concentration—not to mention nerves of steel—to pilot around the track.

Mansell and Piquet (shown) drove the FW11 and its improved B derivative for the 1986 and 1987 seasons (a lifetime in Formula 1). The latter saw the debut of new technology—notably "active suspension" on the FW11B. *Autosport/LAT*

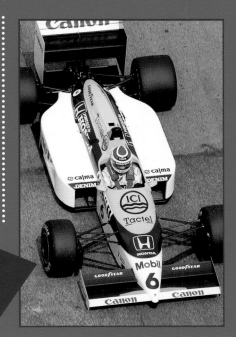

INDEX